Status of Indian Women

A Historical Perspective

JWP PUBLICATIONS

Status of Rural Women in India	75.00
Status of Nurses of India	60.00
Status of Women in the Quran (Urdu)	5.00
Status of Single Women in India	125.00
Status of Banjara Women	125.00
Trafficking in Women and Children in India	125.00
Women in Organised Movements	45.00
Child Labour in Bangalore City	30.00
A Socio-Economic Survey of Slum Dwellers in Calcutta	15.00
Women's Decade (An Assessment)	30.00
The Problem of Dowry in Bangalore City	5.00
Indian Women in Media	12.00
Women and Law	5.00
Prostitution with Religious Sanction (Devadasi/Jogini)	20.00
Changes in Christian Personal Laws	3.50
Christian Marriage and the Customary Practices in Manipur	15.00
The Shahbano Controversy	125.00
Women in CNI Diocese of Delhi	5.00
Wake Up and Live	5.00
Female Sexuality in Hinduism	10.00
Women's Participation in Political Parties in U.P. (Hindi)	250.00
Women in the Freedom Struggle (Hindi)	25.00
Authority of the Religions and the Status of Women	50.00
Pavement Dwellers of Calcutta	15.00
Cultural Chotanagpur: Unity in Diversity	175.00
The Legalization of Prostitution	60.00

Status of Women Series

STATUS OF INDIAN WOMEN
A Historical Perspective

B. R. Sharan

Foreword
D.K. Bhatt
Deputy Commissioner of Police
Crime (Women)
New Delhi

Under the Auspices of
Joint Women's Programme
and
I.S.P.C.K.

UPPAL PUBLISHING HOUSE
NEW DELHI 110 002

UPPAL PUBLISHING HOUSE
3 Ansari Road, Daryaganj, New Delhi 110 002

for

William Carey Study and Research Centre
14/2/ Sudder Street, Calcutta 700 016
and
Joint Women's Programme

ISBN 81-85565-02-3

Printed in India

Published by Uppal Publishing House
3, Ansari Road, Daryaganj, New Delhi-2.
Printed at Mehra Offset Press, New Delhi.

Dedicated

to

Saroj

D. K. Bhatt
Deputy Commissioner of Police
Crime (Women)
Police Hqrs., New Delhi

FOREWORD

There have been a number of books written on the issues and problems pertaining to women in India. The present book "Status of Indian Women a Historical Perspective" is an attempt to see the condition and suffering of women from historical perspective and therefore, the author has chosen a canvas as vast from the ancient times to the present day. Though it is not possible to include each and every aspect of such a vexatious issue agitating the human mind right from the day human relations came into existence and continue to confront the modern day social thinkers. The problem has been dealt with very lucidly and the author has attempted to communicate his point of view very effectively.

The present exercise, is an outcome of prolonged observations, some time participant, some time non-participant, made the author study this topic. Woman has been described/narrated in our philosophy, mythology, religion, whose role has been intermingling depending upon the situation, circumstances of the particular period of history. The author has maintained his focus keeping his object in mind. It is the passion of the author which speaks through the pages. Be it the glorious days of our history where humanity found its dignity/respect in the honour of women. Traversing the path, the author has ruthlessly described the upheavals of history which are largely responsible for a total collapse and degeneration of values for denying her place.

The process through which we have been trying to approach the problem is not unique in the Indian context. This is what the author makes us believe giving out details of women's predicament in Europe at different point of time. And one agrees with the author when he says that uniqueness about Indian context is that though we are approaching half a century of Independence, we still have deaths taking place under the head 'dowry' — a disease which is a deadlier than any thinkable ailment. What we need in the circumstances is not only to fight out the evil of dowry, but a system and support structure to be built up for enquiring into the problems arising out of marital discords. It is the prime need of the hour that we must take a dispassionate look at the problem to reach the malady in order to rectify it. The book has been written with tremendous amount of conviction and passion, a topic very dear to the heart of the author which is reflected throughout the pages of the book. It is hoped that the book will provide sufficient material to the understanding of psycho, sociological, economic aspects related to it.

16.8.1991 **D. K. Bhatt**

Preface

"Status of Indian Women — A Historical Perspective" is an effort to trace the development of the status of women through the pages of history. Mr. Sharan has tried to analyse the different stages of women's development and has attempted to look at the subject from the perspective of a modern Indian gentelman, today.

While accepting the need for women to become equal partners with men in every field, he seems to uphold the view that women were better off in ancient times as wives and mothers, devis and apsaras than they are today.

Mr. Sharan admits that some of the traditions have developed into anti women customs and hopes that while struggling to change them, modern western values should not influence Indian women so much as to take away the essence of the 'Bharatiya Nari'. He wants all concerned people to search for a solution - justice to women, within the Indian heritage and tradition.

Jyotsna Chatterji
Additional Director
Joint Women's Programme

INTRODUCTION

Here is a minor attempt to ameliorate the condition of the sweet and gentle Indian woman. For a long time women everywhere in the world have been struggling for a change in their status. Now with the advent of atomic energy, landing of man on the moon and even taking photos of Neptune's moon Triton, mankind has certainly made greater advancement in technology in the last half century than in any other corresponding period in history, yet one cannot say that betterment in social sphere has kept pace with technical advancement.

We, in India, have no doubt moved forward in the last forty years. In our case, whereas in some fields there has been rapid progress, in some it has been slow and tardy. However, in the case of our women the outcome is at variance. A small segment of them has certainly advanced, but this advancement has been very toilsome. On the other hand, there is the emergence of certain ugly facets in our social order which can at the least be termed as repulsive, with the blame primarily falling on the Indian male. It is surprising that in a country like India which has the most thorough researches done in the discipline of sociology, where meticulous investigations had been done in the field of sex as borne out by the age-old texts of *Kamashastra* and one is today shy to dwell on the problems relating to women.

There is no Kinsey Report in India and efforts made in this respect may not succeed because those interviewed, whether men or women, are not likely to reveal the truth. The least, therefore, we can do is to find out as to what was the state of our women in ancient times, how they stood up to and went through the ordeals during the times of various invasions on our land which resulted in our slavery and what their life is today. We should also have a look at the measures taken up by other societies to improve the lot of their women and examine which of the steps taken up so far have brought social contentment and which have led to chaos. Only then would we be able to formulate what means we should adopt for the betterment of our women and thereby of the whole society.

I have quoted extensively some past masters in diverse fields. The reasons are simple. First, I do not wish the reader to get the impression that these are whims of my fancy or figments of imagination. Secondly, as we all know, human mind reacts differently when it encounters praise or criticism from his own clan or from one considered to be an alien. The words may be the same but depending upon the source one looks for the reasons to reject or accept them. As my aim is higher, to help the fair sex anywhere, I wish to remain clear of such a controversy lest it may mess up my humble effort. I hope that in the process some of the grand works of yesteryears will get a revival or rebirth. Also our attention will be drawn to some recent research work on our sociology done outside India by non-Indians.

I seek the forgiveness of those whom I have quoted or of their publishers for not taking their prior permission. This indiscretion has been exercised for the general good. If desired, I will delete any references with an apology. And then, I also seek the pardon of those reverend intellectuals who consider it a disservice to women or religion if grostque perverted sexual tortures, pointed out by historians or scholars centuries back or now, are put in print. It is my submission that the resultant revulsion caused by such exposures is likely to prove more helpful to our women's cause as some of them are still being subjected to to gory ordeals.

Before we draw any conclusions, we may like to remember that if despite all the tribulations, as brought out in the book, the Western social order still survives, it is to a large extent due to the struggle and ability of the Western educated woman to stand on her feet. What about India, where today ninty per cent of the women are uneducated and at the present rate of progress a large percentage will remain so for the next 200 years? Our actions should be directed towards their uplift. Let the miniscule minority of the advanced women, who know what is good for them, find their own way. For the rest, the thought of instantly achieving total sexual freedom is likely to bring ruination and that has to be averted.

Finally, I would like to express my sincere thanks to Mr. Ram Swaroop, Mr. Yves de Saint-Jacob, and Mrs. Jyotsna Chatterji, all intellectual giants, for their open comments and most valuable advice.

B. R. Sharan

CONTENTS

1

CONCEPT OF LOVE

In a vast country like ours it is natural that different views are expressed on various issues. On the important question relating to women's rights, individual orthodox views are expressed which cut across all political or religious barriers. One finds people condoning the burning of a young widow; some advocate denial of subsistence to her; others would like that a woman must allow herself to be overburdened with unwanted children even if that means virtual death to her when alive. In protest, different women's groups have been formed, primarily in major cities, to put up the case for the advancement of their gender. Their activities are generally confined to voicing their rights to live with dignity. No demonstrations have been organised by them so far demanding right to live as lesbians or as unwed mothers nor is there any cry for freedom to have free sex. The only active demonstrations ever held are against rape or for social and economic justice demanding a rightful place in society.

It is heartening to note that more forward looking thoughts are being advocated by some men. No one has in the recent past given a call for advancement more vigorously than the eminent Mr. Vasant Sathe. We shall go through a few excerpts from his recent article, "*The Love Bug Strikes—Sex, Sex and more Sex*", to see whether what is advocated by him should be accepted in totality. Mr. Sathe says:

"Now, in a village... you will find that people have better knowledge of sex than the urban middle-class. Because they learn from nature. Now, knowledge is very essential: It takes away ignorance, inhibitions and wrong notions...

"The human being is the only creature which has intelligence. As far as the animal world is concerned, they're all regulated by nature. There is no rape in animals. There is no homosexuality. Human beings, because they have minds, can think of all the perverse things...

"I think the medieval ages, particularly after the onslaught of Brahmanical orthodoxy and Islamic invasions, have contributed to the current orthodoxy about sex. The breaking away from the earlier freedom, knowledge and education...

"A time has come when all these inhibitions must be removed. They're there in our society, subconsciously, particularly among the middle class. Even the so-called upper class, just because they're rich or they're the elite, are not really liberated or educated...

"For nearly a thousand years it has been injected in people's minds that sex is something sinful. Sex (*sambhog*) particularly out of marriage is absolutely sinful. This has sort of cast a spell on the minds of our young people. Total inhibition. I think we need to bring them out of this orthodoxy and suppression... That togetherness has nothing to do with marriage. Marriage is an institution created by man for social stability. Fine. But physical union, coming together, has nothing to do with institutionalising...

"In western society...you will find that for the youth there, sex is more an act of adventurous rebellion towards orthodoxy. Thus, they have swung to the other extreme of trying to be libertine. This again has made them neurotic. This has caused more harm to the youth in that society because they did not have the concept of harmony, of equilibrium, of synthesis, of balance, which was inherent in our culture..." [1]

---

1 *The Illustrated Weekly of India*, 21-27 June, 1987.

In one single stroke Mr Sathe has made the effort to push India into the 21st century in the field of sex.In one single stroke, he has thrown to the winds the grand work of Mahatma Gandhi — "Self–Indulgence vs Self-Restraint" — teaching us abstinence which, though not totally possible, at least helped us keep the blood in the vessels under reasonably controlled circulation.

By this one single stroke Mr. Sathe has perhaps tried to uplift the uninitiated and unenlightened into the harmonic deathlock of free *sambhog*. He says that it is the middle class that is engulfed in the cobwebs of sexual inhibitions, perhaps, meaning thereby that the poor people below the poverty line have at least cut across any such barrier. Will this latter class, say fifty per cent of our people, accept this stigma that sex is free in their milieu? He then says that even the so called upper class is not really liberated. If the poor have been too low to observe any moral code, the rich have always been everywhere in the world too high to succumb to any such ethical pressure or virtuous pretensions. It is a strange land, this dear country of ours. The majority of its people are poor but the poor are themselves divided into two distinctly discernible classes, the havenots and the lowest among low. The former are larger in number; the majority of them, with means just bare enough to let them subsist, take as much pride in their hoary past and are as much conservative in their social outlook as the most orthodox genre of the middle class. Inter-class rivalry may find its expression in any other field, but in the matter of sex, the havenots have not only retained their obduracy but not allowed the scintillating path of sexual freedom to pave the way for their economic progress.

As for the lowliest, in reality, we are witnessing a strange phenomenon. As economic conditions improve for them they tend to adopt discriminatory conservative values held by the other classes. Most of the lower class women work in order to subsist.

As the husband starts earning a little more, he desires that the woman is withdrawn in his shell, as a status symbol to be shown to his community, denied any opportunity to expose herself and thus made incapable of finding her rightful place. There is no desire to educate her. Future positive changes in the position of our women are thus likely to proceed haltingly and unevenly. Should we then allow our inevitable economic progress to further minimise the chances of our young girls of having the benefit of new opportunities which our boys are able to grasp in plenty?

We are now told that it has been injected in our people's mind that sex, particularly out of marriage, is absolutely sinful. We know that the enlightened West has already moved far too forward in this field. Let us, therefore, see as to how they have been through the life-line. For this exercise to be fruitful, one cannot think of sex in isolation. As Gandhiji advised: "The whole gamut of man's activities today constitutes an indivisible whole. You cannot divide social, political and purely religious work into water tight compartments..."[2] Plato (427-327 BC) also, in his well known dialogue, *The Symposium*, in which a group of banquet guests discuss ideal love and beauty, tries to accentuate the disastrous effects of this tendency of compartmentalisation of human faculties, occupations and spheres of activity. Therefore, the whole subject should be viewed in totality and only then we should decide on our future course.

---

2 Radhakrishnan, Ed., *Mahatma Gandhi*, p.105; *Gandhi and Social Sciences*, Bookhive, New Delhi, 1970, p.22.

2

THE YOODHISTRA ERA

Serious efforts have been made by European nations to study the course of human development. Hermann Ploss says, "Hardly any student or investigator with claims to serious consideration can doubt that we have developed and evolved into what we now are not only somatically but sociologically and culturally. Moreover, the evolution of the more complex forms of life out of the simpler one has not been a direct, even oblique, ascent, but a wave-like succession of achievements and relapses, a spiral with occasional sharp forward spurts. In order to grasp fully the course of human evolution we need to know much more: first of all of recorded history, as well as pre-history, in which the most significant factors were frequently ignored, either because their significance was overlooked, or beacuse it was deliberately suppressed for reasons of traditional morality or political utility. A further source of valuable material, if taken in continuous conjunction and comparison with modern ethnology, is study of myths and legends". [1]

In our effort to have a forward jump, we should not base our thesis on surmises that have no foundation. We no doubt have a galore of myths and legends but we are not so primitive that our recorded history, or even pre-history for that matter, cannot substantiate what our society stood for.

---

[1] *Woman*, A historical, gynaecological and anthropological compendium. Hermann Heinrich Ploss, Max Bartels, and Paul Bartels, William Heinemann (Medical Books) Ltd., 1935. Printed in England by Whitefriars Press Ltd., London, 1935; vol i, p.457. Some observations quoted on European society are based on the authority of this compendium.

It is not that the middle ages, particularlarly after the onslaught of Brahmanical orthodoxy and Islamic invasions, have contributed to the current orthodoxy about sex. Where was the earlier free style? The earliest Epic that gives us detailed idea of our people's attitude towards sex is the *Ramayana*, which is of a time much earlier than the medieval period. Had we ever been uninhibited Mother Sita would not have been put through the fire test by Lord Rama himself.

One of the earliest eras known to us is the Yoodhistra era. Col. James Tod says: "Having regained his kingdom, he proclaimed a new era and placing on the throne of Indraprastha, Parikhita, grandson to Arjuna, retired to Dwarica with Crishna and Baldeva".[2]

According to the authentic chronicle of the age, *Rajatarangini* of 1740 A.D., "Since the War (*Mahabharata*) to the period of writing, 4636 years have elapsed". That means Yoodhishtra established his era 2896 years before Christ.

Col. Tod, however, investigated further and says :

"I venture to place the establishment in India proper of these two grand races, distinctively called those of *Soorya* (Sun) and *Chandra* (Moon) at about 2256 years before the Christian era; at which period, though somewhat later, the Egyptian, Chinese, and Assyrian monarchies are generaly stated to have been established, and about a century and a half after the great event, the Flood. (Egyptian, under Misraim, B.C. 2188; Assyrian, 2059; Chinese, 2207)." [3]

---

2 *Annals and Antiquities of Rajasthan*, 1820, vol. i., p. 43.

3 Tod, op.cit., vol.i, p.32.

What is relevant here is that Yoodhishtra retired to Dwarika in the *Dwapar age*. The Hindus have divided the life of mankind into four ages. Of the first, *Satyug*, the age of eternal truth, not much historical evidence is available. Of the second, *Treta*, synonymous with Lord Rama, authentic archival testimony is available across the land. The first epic known to mankind was written in Rama's age by Valmiki. And *Dwapar*, with which Lord Krishna and Yoodhishtra are associated, was an age posterior to Lord Rama's. Some zealots of course would like to heap ages upon ages to our history and question as to how it can be that there was no era before Yoodhistra? Even if there was, and Yoodhishtra era was not the first, is it of much consequence today whether another era had started 5000 or 7000 years back? On the other hand supposing one instituted a Gandhian era when we became independent in 1947, would it mean that our civilisation would be abridged to less than a century, making us forget all that we were earlier or thereafter? What is relevant is that we go through available records, see the good and the bad in them and then formulate our code for social conduct for the general good.

3

THE FAIR SEX IN EARLIER INDIA

To understand our cultural ethos in its entirety we shall have to go back to the earliest women known to us. No better tribute has been paid to them than by that grand British lady, Annie Besant, who came to India in 1893 and by her dauntless work was elevated to the highest post of the President of the Indian National Congress by the Indian people in 1917. On Indian women she wrote: Literature can show no grander type of womanhood than are to be found in the great epic peoms of India, types sketched in by master hands from noble models, and uniting in a few heroic figures all that is at once strongest and sweetest, most lofty and most devoted in humanity..." [1]

There is no better criterion of the refinement of the nation than the condition of the fair sex there. The more civilised a people, the more recognition they give to their women and a stage comes as expressed by Comte Ségur, when "*Les hommes font les lois, les femmes font les moeurs.*" (Men make laws, women the manners).[2] The manners of a people, says the celebrated Goguet, "always bear a proportion to the progress they have made in the arts and sciences", and Tod queries, "Where can we look for sages like those (except in India) whose systems of philosophy were the prototypes of those of Greece: to whose works Plato, Thales, and Pythagoras were disciples? Where shall we find the astronomers whose knowledge of the planetary system yet excites wonder in Europe, as well as the architects and sculptors whose works claim our admiration, and the musicians, who could make the mind oscillate from joy to sorrow, from tears to smiles with the change

---

[1] *New York World*, 3 June 1896.

[2] *Les femmes, leur conditions et leur influence dans l'ordre sociale*, Tod, op.cit., vol. i, p.10.

of modes and varied intonation... The influence of women is marked in every page of Hindu history, from the most remote periods. What led to the wars of Rama ? The abduction of Sita. What rendered deadly the feuds of the Yadus? The insult to Draupadi. What made prince Nala an exile from Nirwur? His love for Damyanti. What made Raja Bhirtri abandon the throne of Awinti? The loss of Pingani. What subjected the Hindu to the domination of the Islamite? The abduction of the princess of Canouj. In fine, the cause which overturned kingdoms, commuted the sceptre to the pilgrim's staff and found the groundwork of all their grand epics, is woman". [3]

In the Hindu legend, Vishnu is the Supreme God, the preserver of the Universe. Two other Lords, Brahma, the creator and Siva, the destroyer, together form the Trinity with the Almighty that governs all the worlds. Brahma is said to have sprung from the lotus, the symbol of fertility, in the naval of Vishnu; Siva is hailed to have been born from the forehead of Brahma. That Vishnu and Siva have temples dedicated to them in each village of India, and Brahma has only one temple for him at Pushkar, made as late as in early nineteenth century, is a mystery more so as Puskhar remains till today the sole tabernacle dedicated to him. One legend is that Brahma decided to perform a *yagna* for the creation of mankind at Pushkar. The sacred fire for the *yagna* was fast running out, but Saraswati, Brahma's wife, was still getting dressed up for the occasion. The auspicious time for the *Yagna* was kindled but as the rites could not be performed without a female, Brahma formed Gayatri, a young girl to take Saraswati's place. The latter on arrival was enraged at finding another taking her position and went off to Ratnagiri hill leaving behind the curse that this would be the only locale on earth where Brahma would be worshipped. Today those who worship Brahma at Pushkar also pay their obeisance to the goddess.

[3] Tod. op.cit, vol.i, pp.481, 501.

So much for the power the better half had even before the Creator could put mankind fully in its cradle. What is worthwhile noting is that whereas the other two Lords of the Trinity are always worshipped in accompaniment of their fair partners yet each one of the Trinity's spouse is worthy enough on her own to demand singular devotion. Laxmi, the symbol of prosperity, the consort of the supreme Vishnu, is worshipped without Him at the great festival of *Diwali* (alongwith Ganesa, the elephant-headed son of Siva, the remover of all obstacles invoked at the beginning of all undertakings). Saraswati, the personification of intelligence, demands attention alone without her discarded partner, Brahma. Unaccompanied Parvati is worshipped as the powerful *Durga*, *Kali* or *Shakti*, and even after her fragmented body was scattered to immortality throughout the land by her associate Siva himself, each of her parts, including the one that demands absolute privacy, is idolised separately. And then two incarnations blessed our land. First came Lord Rama, whose act demands total respect and yet the enquiring mind fails to reconcile with the sufferings that his consort had to go through.

Janaki, maiden Sita, was the exalted princess to seek whose fair hand all the powerful lords from distant lands assembled at her *Syamvara*—a ceremony to which all eligible suitors were invited out of whom the maiden chose one. Before a prince could even dream of the coveted garland being put around his neck, he had to qualify by physically lifting the heavy immovable bow of Lord Siva. How such a delicate flower herself forced her way to oblivion just to keep company with her exiled husband, Rama, surpasses all comprehension. Tod pays his homage, "Do we desire to see a model of unbounded devotion, resignation, and love, let us take the picture of Sita, as painted by the Milton of their silver age, than which nothing more beautiful or sentimental may be culled even from *Paradise Lost.* Rama was about to abandon his faithful wife for the purpose of becoming a *Venaprest'ha* or hermit, when she thus pours out her ardent desire to partake of his solitude:

" A woman's bliss is found, not in the smile
of father, mother, friend, nor in herself:
Her husband is her only portion here,
Her heaven hereafter. If thou indeed
Depart this day into the forest drear,
I will precede, and smooth the thorny way.

A gay recluse
On thee attending, happy shall I feel
Within the honey-scented grove to roam,
For thou e'en here canst nourish and protect;
And therefore other friend I cannot need.
Today most surely with thee will I go,
And thus resolved, I must not be deny'd.
Roots and wild fruit shall be my constant food;
Nor will I near thee add unto thy cares,
Nor lag behind, nor forest - food refuse
But fearless traverse every hill and dale.

Thus could I sweetly pass a thousand years;
But without thee even heaven would lose its charms.

Pleased to embrace thy feet, I will reside
In the rough forest as my father's house.
Void of all other wish, supremely thine,

Permit me this request — I will not grieve.
I will not burden thee — refuse me not.
But shouldst thou, Raghuvu, this prayer deny
Know, I resolve on death."

– Vide Ward [4]

---

[4] *On the History, Literature, and Mythology of the Hindus*, vol. ii, p.408; Tod, op.cit, vol. i, pp. 487-88.

And yet such a noble soul had to go through the fire test to prove her purity in captivity. The imagery Valmiki uses on the occasion — of fire-ordeal in Lanka—is very subtle. Rama tells Sita: "When you, whose chastity is overcast by the shadow of misgiving, stand near me, it offends my eyes even as a lamp affects a man of sore eyes. The flame is not sickly, it burns bright; it is the eyes that look upon it that are sick..."

Much later, when the Royal steed was being prepared to wander around the whole land, heralding the advent of the unchallengeable upright rule all throughout, Rama preferred to quieten a single wayward tongue and banish his dearest consort Sita. His own fidelity remained unquestionable, but what was the crime of the innocent spotless Sita who had already been put

And then shone a new light.

Lord Krishna was husband of 16, 108 wives, each one better than the other and flowered them with simultaneous and equal attention. Yet not one of them was high enough to demand worship alongside the Lord, not even Rukmani, the most respected and seniormost consort. This merit stays with a companion, the eternal Radha, whose name has graced millions of maidens, more than any other name around the Universe. She was only a *gopi*, an ardently devoted nymph, a muse inspiring poetic inspiration, older than the little Lord, whose love begot divine harmony.

Inquisitiveness of ignorant minds gets jumbled up when one learns that Radha was not married to Krishna. At a time when modern society is discarding the concept of Platonic love as a myth, how is one to understand Radha, the personification of that unending ocean of love that generates total adherence for her in every heart? She demands our worship, for her love was sublime in purity. That she ranks together on the same pedestal that adorns the mercurial Almighty is a befitting tribute that millions pay to her; for she, in her affectionate devotion, expected no reward in return except a propitious glimpse of Krishna, the most beloved Lord of any Hindu maiden.

We are advised that myths and legends of the primitive people are a source of valuable material. Let us have a look at a leaf taken out of this gold–mine, pertaining to the age of Krishna, by the erudite Tod and see how 'primitive' we have been.

"Vyas, the author of the grand epic *the Mahabharata*, [5] was son of Santana (of the race of Heri), sovereign of Delhi, by Yojnaganda, a fisherman's daughter, [6] consequently illegitimate. He became the spiritual father, or preceptor, of his nieces, the daughters of Vichitravira, the son and successor of Santana. Vichitravira had no male offspring. Of his three daughters, one... being by a slave, it was necessary to ascertain which a difficult matter from the seclusion in which they were kept. It was therefore left to Vyasu to discover the pure of birth; who determined that nobility of blood would show itself, and commanded that the princesses should walk uncovered before him. The elder, from shame, closed her eyes, and from her was born the blind Dhertarashtra, ... the second, from the same feeling, covered herself with yellow ochre, called *Pandu*, and henceforth she bore the name of Pandea, and her son was called Pandu; while the third stepped forth unabashed. She was abjudged not of gentle blood, and her issue was Vidura." [7]

---

5 "See translation of this epic, by Messrs. Carey and Marshman."

6 "It is a very curious circumstance, that Hindu legend gives to two of their most celebrated authors, whom they have invested with a sacred character, a descent from the aboriginal and impure tribes of India: Vyasu from a fisherman, and Valmika, the author of the other grand epic *the Ramayana*, from *budhek* or robber, an associate of the Bhil tribe at Aboo..." (Tod, *op.cit.*, vol.i., p.25).

7 Tod, op.cit., vol. i, p.26. Vidura, a *sudra*, stands for *Buddhi*. (wisdom), the one-pointed reason. As prime-minister he played a distinguished role in *the Mahabharata*.

Coming to King Pandu, we find rare instances in our mythology which thrives on highlighting all conceivable facets of life. Let us take the cases of the two most important female characters in *the Mahabharata*. Kunti was married to Pandu, who, it is said, fell a victim to a curse given by a begetter in ecstasy who was unwittingly killed by Pandu's arrow in a hunt. Pandu was denied the power of insemination or face death as a consequence. Earlier, due to a charm given to Kunti by the sage Durvasa, Karna was begotten straight from the Sun-god even before her wedlock. She had no option but to hide this fact which she regretted throughout. Then, as Pandu was not being blessed with progeny, she enticed the deities from their spheres. To *Dharma Raj* (Minos) she bore Yoodishtra, by *Pavan* (Eolus) she had Bhima and by *Indra* (Jupiter Coelus) she had Arjuna. To help Madri, Pandu's second wife, Kunti gave her part of her boon and Nycula and Sydeva were the twin sons of Madri by *Aswini Kumar* (Esculapius) the physician of the gods.

Let us see what Dr. Annie Besant has to say on Kunti: "You find women like Kunti—we say about 5000 years ago (3000 BC) but Orientalists in the West will put the date at a later period, some 1500 or 1000 years before Christ—and Kunti was a mother of heroes. You remember how she said when she heard that the day of the battle was approaching: 'This is the day for which a *kshatriya* woman bears her sons. Go forth and fight. ' It recalls the Japanese woman, held up as a example of patriotism so often, who when she was found weeping, her sons having perished in war, and sympathy for their death was proffered, turned around and said: 'I am not weeping because my sons are dead. I am weeping that I have no more sons to give to the service of the country.' Such a woman was Kunti, the mother of the Pandavas, and she was not alone..."[8]

---

8 *Indian Woman*, p.55

Later, the acquired prize of Draupadi won in a *syamvara* by Arjuna, was gifted to all Pandava sons inadvertently by Kunti. Such was the honour given to a mother [9] that to keep her words, all the five brothers accepted Draupadi as a common wife much against the prevalent order. Perhaps they had no regrets because they had all the options, later exercised, to marry separately. As for Draupadi, she could see through all her five powerful husbands because her unplanned and unheard of polyandry was systemised as she was available to only one at a time till a child was born. Yet the incident resulted in such insults being hurled at her that to redeem her honour, the Pandavas had to wage the greatest war of the age.

A Western school of thought says, "Polygamy and polyandry were practised by the ancients in a mistaken view of the animal economy, and of the first great command to people the earth; the one was general amongst all nations of antiquity; the other rare, though to be found in Scythia, India and even amongst the Natches, in the new world..."[10] One may safely clarify that despite Kunti and Draupadi finding an honourable place in one of the top religious archives, polyandry itself has no place anywhere in India (except in odd hill tribes) that the Indians know of, whereas it did exist in some other societies as in Britain in the days of Caesar. The accurate writer, speaking of the natives of that island, says, "*Uxores habent deni-dupoenique inter se communes, et maxime fratres cum fractribus, parentesque cum liberis; sed si qui sint ex his nati, eorum habentur liberi, quo primum virgo quaeque deducta est.* As strange medley of polyndary and polygamy!" observes Tod, [11] without enlightening the reader with a handy translation.

---

[9] 'The mother and the motherland are greater than heaven' is the Indian attitude from the earliest times. *Janani Janambhumisca swargadapi gariyasi..*

[10] Tod, op.cit., vol.i., p.485.

[11] Tod, op.cit., vol.i. p.70.

We have, however, been able to get another version which describes the state of affairs more clearly.

In Britain at the time of Roman invasion in 55 and 54 B.C., De Bello Gallio records in *Caesar*, (Julius, 100-44 B.C.), "They have their wives in common, 10 or 12 together, mostly fraternally or as between father and sons. The children borne by the woman are counted as children of the man who knew her first".[12] Among the Nordic and Teutonic races there are records of other primitive customs, indicating past phases of developments: the practice of burning the widow on the husband's pyre and the right of the man to bequeath, sell and give away or lend his wife. [13] Till recently the position of women in the West was hardly praiseworthy. Sir P.S. Sivaswami Iyer gives quotations to show their ill-treatment and that till comparatively recent times women in England could be beaten with a stick by their husbands. [14]

According to Hindu narration, in the beginning Brahma, the Lord of Beings, created men and women. Rules for regulating their existence with regard to *dharma* (a comprehensive term which includes law, religion, morality, righteousness, duty , benevolence etc.), *artha* (worldly wealth) and *kama* (love, pleasure or sexual gratifiation) were laid down in the form of commandments in one hundred thousand chapters divided into four divisions. The original *Veda. Sruti* directly heard from God by the *rishis*, was passed down from mouth to mouth. Some of these chapters which dealt with *dharma* were codified much later as *Smritis* separately by Swayambhuva Manu, who belonged to the period of the Epic Age

---

[12] *Woman*, op.cit., vol. i, p.524.

[13] K. Weinhold, *Die Deutchen Frauen in Mittelalter*, Wein, 1882; Woman, vol.i.,p.530.

[14] *Evolution of Hindu Moral Ideals*, Kamla Lectures, 1935, pp.52-65;V. Raghavan, *The Culture Heritage of India*, op.cit., vol.ii., p.354.

which produced the *Ramayana* and the *Mahabharta*; those that related to *artha* were compiled by Brahspati and those that referred to *kama* were expounded by Nandi, the follower of Siva, in one thousand chapters. *Dharma* sustained society and on it were based the other two vital activities of *artha* and *kama* which had to be carried on within the outer limits of *dharma*. Lord Krishna himself declared, *Dharma viruddho bhuteshukamosmi* (I am pleasure, *Kama*, unopposed to *dharma*)[15] The *Vedas* are *apauruseya*, not man-made and were therefore, self-atuthoritative, needing no external support. The *Smritis* on the other hand are man-made; yet they are authoritative only because they come from men with profound knowledge of the *Vedas*. In the case of a contradiction between a *Vedic* text and *Smriti*, the *Vedic* text is supposed to prevail.

It is a pity that no book of the Indian history till now teaches our girls as to what was the position of our women in the beginning of the things and as to how and why they have been brought to be what they are today. Regular historical composition was an art not unknown to Ancient India. In the course of various invasions our records were burnt with as little mercy to literary treasures as Omar displayed towards the Alexanderine library. Some of the valuable material that was left is either still kept secret at a few ancient temples or was sent to the dead archives of the Royal Asiatic society in London for further research! [16] Tod, who himself indulged in this activity, however, does bring out a shortcoming, "Yet from *the Mahabharata*, or Great War, to Alexander's invasion, and from that great event to the era of Mahmood of Ghazni, scarcely a paragraph of pure native Hindu history (except as before started) has hitherto been revealed to the curiosity of western scholars !"[17] Most history books talk of the

---

[15] *Bhagwad Gita* vii.ii.

[16] Tod, op.cit., vol.i, p.1.

[17] Tod, op.cit., vol.i, p.2.

'greatness' of various rulers including some of our own, without bringing out as to how at each stage thety took steps, which resulted in a decline in the status of our women, It ofcourse suited the invaders' historians to prove that the natives' social life needed improvement which they alone could take care of. This, however, should not now come in the way of our history books teaching our children our actual heritage in its correct perspective.

Some remarkable efforts have been made by foreign historians like Abul Fazil, who wrote *Outlines of Ancient Hindu History*, Wilson, Wilkins, Schlegel and Tod to quote a few, to reveal some of the hidden lore of India. Indian historians in their research work have unfortunately been constrained to rely only on such works which could not but be subjective. Yet, the early Westerners must be given the credit for bringing out some other aspects of the greatness of ancient India. In peninsular India, 459 prehistoric sites, among which 42 belonged to the old Stone Age and 252 to the new, were located between 1863 and 1904. These sites have thrown up new light on the age of early man in India when implements and weapons were made of stone and not metal. The inhabitants had then learnt how to make pottery and discovered the use of potter's wheel, one of the earliest of human inventions. We have not yet found a habitation used by early man in India nor so far his skeletal remains; we do not know who were the makers of the caves in Kurnool and Alicoor in South India belonging to this period and what kind of life they led. Some of the burials in which large blocks of stone were erected on graves in India in the early Metal Ages may have already started in the earlier Neolithic times. More work is required to get the details of this age as has been done in Western Europe.

The discoveries of Harappa and Mohenjo-daro made in the twenties of this century, have revealed that in the third millennium B.C. as estimated by Western archivists, a full fledged Indus Valley civilisation of Indian origin flourished which rightfully gave

India, "an important place among the countries of the most ancient East".[18] From the finds at the sites, communication by sea, river and overland is established not only with the rest of India but also all the regions of the Middle-East. As for arts and crafts, the findings of various forms of jewellary made of gold and silver studded with precious stones, bronze [19] statuette of a nude girl well adorned, a nude male figure carved in red sandstone and another in dark grey slate, the *lingams* and *yonis* and of a god bedecked with much jewellery in the *urdhvamedhra* (penis eructus form), which Sir John Marshall considered to be a prototype of historic Siva in his Pasupathi aspect,[20] amply demonstrate that it could not be too closed minded a society. Briefly, the religion of the Indus people consisted in worshipping the Mother Goddess, the prototype of Siva, the phallic symbols, the *swastika* etc. The skeletal material reveals four different racial types. These are Austroloid, Austric or Austo-Asiatic (*Nisadas*), who came from West and are now represented by the tribes like the Kolas and Mundas living in central and eastern India; the Mongoloid or Sino-Tibetan branch cf the Alpine stock (*Kiratas*); the Alpine; and the Dravidian (*Dravidas*) who are believed to have come to India from the east Mediterranean region through Iran long before the Aryans showing that it was the meeting ground of several races. "It is very interesting to note," remarked Rawlinson, "that there existed in Sind, 5000 years ago, cities which were in may respects far in advance of many Indian cities of today."[21]

---

[18] V.Gordon Childe, *New Light On The Most Advanced East*, Routlege and Kegan Paul, 2nd Ed., London, 1952.

[19] Alloy of tin and copper. Iron was already much in use.

[20] Sir John Marshall, *Mohenjo-daro and the Indian Civilisation*, vol.i., pp.39-40.

[21] H. G. Rawlinson. C.I.E., M.A., F.R. Hist. S.A. Concise History of the Indian People (First Published in 1938), Seventh Impression, 1968, p.11.

The Aryans came to India, as per Western historians, in the second millenium B.C. bringing with them a new culture. There seems to be a marked dissimilarity in several important facets of life between the Aryans and the Indus people. Till the Mohenjo-daro script is deciphered any proper evaluation is bound to remain dubious. From present day knowledge it appears that the destruction of the Harappan civilisation was brought about by the Aryans at about 1500 B.C.

In early *Vedic* society, from all available accounts, women occupied the same position as men. Complete gender equality is found in all parts of *Vedic* literature. Women reached a very high standard of learning and culture and made all-round progress. They could move freely with their husbands or lovers and followed a number of professions. Some of the Vedic poets were women; the *Rig-Veda*, the oldest known scripture in the whole world, contains hymns (*suktas*) by as many as twenty-seven women. Some of these hymns are frank expressions of their inner, womanly desire for a worthy loving husband, a happy and prosperous home-life free from co-wives and so on. Literary scholars like Godha, Ghosa, Vishwahara, Apalla, Rousha and others were well known and acknowledged for their intellectual and literary abilities. The *Mahabharata* describes in detail several women scholars like Shiva, Shandih, Shuvravathi, Sulma, Dhararini, Naina, Vedavathi etc. Women in the age of Panini (fifth century B.C.) continued the *Vedic* tradition of high culture and education. There were women warriors who fought bravely in war. There were also women philosophers. There are some references to hetairae (open concubinage) in the *Vedic* texts. There seems to have been no sort of opprobrium attached to such women. [22] The practice of allowing women to select a husband out of a chosen group rules out the possibility of child marriages. The tie of marriage was a

22 C. Kunhan Raja, *Vedic Culture*, *The Cultural Heritage of India*, op.cit., vol.i, p.214.

binding force all through life. A wife was her husband's help-mate (*sahadharmini*), friend and comrade. A man could not undertake any social or religious duty without his wife. Divorce was not permitted and there is evidence to show that levirate and widow marriages prevailed. *Sati* did not exist in the *Vedic* age. Monogamy was the normal rule but polygamy was permitted and practiced by the rich and the ruling classes. Polyandry was unknown. The family was of patriarchal type. Women had control over their *parinaya* (gifts and property etc. received at the time of the marriage) and it was considered a sin if relatives took away *stridhana* (property exclusively belonging to the wife).

In the very early period, when the Aryans were still moving and had not formed themselves into definite settlements they used to perform all the functions without any differentiation or exact division of functions into classes. We then find the statement in Sanskrit books that the Aryans had grown to be men of three *varnas* (classes) in the Indo-Iranian times. The *brahman* learnt and taught, the *kshatriya* protected and preserved order and the *vaisya* was the custodian of the economic functions of the society. The class formations were not rigid at first. Marriages took place in all the three *varnas* and there was no question of *anuloma* (wife inferior in caste) and *pratiloma* (husband inferior in caste). When the Aryans settled down in the midst of the indigenous Indian population, a fourth class, *sudra*, those outside the original Aryan population who provided manual labour came into being. Marriages took place with the latter and the children were brought up as if they were Aryan. Later the off-springs were given a lower place in the family. Sir P. S. Sivaswami Iyer has brought out that the recognition of mixed marriages—no doubt with decreasing influence and status—went on till it about 1100 A.D. But long before this stage was reached, the mother's class, not father's , became the sole determining factor in fixing the position of the issue. It was the presence and influence of the racial factor in the case of the fourth caste that affected the relations among the first three also. And free intermarriage amongst them came to be governed by the rule of the inferior and superior *anuloma* and *pratiloma*. New names were given to the issue of mixed marriages though a child of a *sudra* woman remained a *sudra*. The father's functions had fixed the son's functions in the earlier times but the mother's caste fixed the son's caste in the latter times. The conception of class was functional in the first period but it became caste in the second.[23] It has been said that caste is a unique and puzzling institution of Hindu India not to be found anywhere else in the world. Surprisingly this degrading system, which was brought into usage when the Aryans invaded India got strengthened when we ourselves were invaded and its corrupting influence has also permeated among other religions that thrive in India. Rigidity, however, cannot be enforced in one field in isolation. Its effects are all-encompassing.

Since Manu was the first who codified the laws, let us take a glimpse of what he said on women. He wisely pronounced, "Where women verily are honoured, there the gods rejoice. Where, however, they are not honoured, there all sacred rites prove useless".[24] And he further declared, "In whatever house a woman not duly honoured pronounces an imprecation, that house, with all that belongs to it shall utterly perish."[25] Somehow, somewhere, while glorifying our women we started taking away all their rights and privileges. "The position of women of India gradually deteriorated as the golden *Vedic* ideals of unity and equality began to fade through the passage of time. During the period of the *Smritis* — the period of codification of social laws — women were bracketed with the *sudras*, and were denied the right to study the *Vedas*... Marriage or domestic life became compulsory for women

---

[23] See T. R. Venkataraman Sastri, C.I.E., *The Smritis: Their Outlook and Character*, The Cultural Heritage of India, vol ii, pp. 324-329.

[24] Manu III. 56.

[25] Manu IX.45.

and unquestioning devotion to, and self–effacing service of husbands their only duty." [26]

There is no doubt that Manu who examined the social aspect laid down a code of conduct for women which today appears strict. Women, ofcourse were protected at home and in society. Brahspati laid down that if a man violated an unwilling woman, his property was to be confiscated and he would be paraded as an ass. For adultery, abandoning of the wife by husband was not advocated by the *Smiriti* writers of the period but she was required to go through appropriate penance. The woman was to be abandoned only if she had conceived as a result of adultery though some later writers opined that she was to be considered impure only till delivery and the illegitimate child was to be handed over to someone else for rearing.[27] Reference to *Punarbhu* (the remarried woman) appear in *Dharam-Sastras*. "When her husband', says Narada (who is generally placed about the early centuries of the Chrishtian era)), "is lost (i.e., gone to no one knows where), or dead, or is impotent or has become a religious ascetic or been expelled from the caste: these are the five cases of legal necessity in which a woman may be justified in taking another husband."[28]

---

[26] Roma Chaudhury, *Some Reflections on the Ideals of Indian Womanhood*, The Cultural Heritage of India, op.cit., vol ii, p.607.
[27] D.C. Ganguly, *Some Aspects of the Position of Women in Ancient India*, The Cultural Heritage of India, op.cit., Vol.ii., p.597.
[28] Narada, *Stripumsa*, St. 97. Cf. *Agni*.P.154.5-6; *The Cultural Heritage of India* op.cit., vol. ii, p. 578.

It is not possible to ascertain the exact period when Manu wrote the *Smritis* . Some say he was contemporary of Kautilya; few maintain he followed Kautilya; others place him much earlier. It would however be of interest to note that there was a sharp and radical disparity of approach between Kautilya and Manu. The former was Minister of Chandragupta Maurya who ruled from 322-298 B.C. Mr. Justice P.B. Gajendragadkar, who later became the Chief Justice of India, has pointed out, "The publication by Dr. Shama Sastri of *Arthasastra* of Kautilya in 1909 in the Mysore Sanskrit Series was an epoch–making event in the history of the research on Hindu law... Kautilya allows *niyoga* (levirate) in its ancient fullness to widows and to wives of men afflicted with disease; Manu condemns it. Kautilya would recoginse the existence of courtesans and would seek to organise them; whereas Manu would punish them as public scourge. Kautilya would attempt to regulate gambling and drink; Manu condemns it as a sin. Kautilya knows of remarried widows and unmarried mothers; Manu would forbid remarriages except in the case of widows who are virgins...Kautilya and Manu differ in regard to shares to be allotted to sisters on inheritance. Kautilya forbids suicide, and disapproves of *sati*, whereas Manu does not seem to renounce *sati* expressly. Kautilya condemns addiction to astrology; Manu would only discourage the pursuit of astrology as a profession... These differences can be satisfactorily explained on the theory that the *Arthasastra* was dealing with secular law... whereas *Dharma-sastra* considered the same problems from an ethical, religious or moral point of view and gave effect to the notions on which Hindu social structure was based."[29] Mr. Gajendragadkar has in this context also

[29] *The Historical Background and Theoritic Basis of Hindu Law, The Cultural Heritage of India*, op.cit., vol.ii, pp. 419-433.

made somc observations which are :-

1. "It appears that Kautilya's *Arthasastra* refers to more than a dozen previous authors on *Arthasastra*... The question which arises for consideration is, did secular-law as expounded in the *Arthasastra* begin to function and progress independently of Hindu law which is to be found in the *Smriti* literature? ... *Arthasastra* had progressed independently of the *Dharam-Sastra* until the present Manu *Smriti* was composed. "(op.cit., p. 429)

2. "Indeed it may be legitimate to say that the very harsh criticism made by Maine against Hindu law must not be regarded as unjustified. 'On the whole', says Maine, 'the impression left on the mind by the study of these books (books on *Dharma-sastra*) is, that a more awful tyrany never existed than this which proceeded from the union of political, intellectual, and spiritual ascendancy.'[30] And he adds that 'Hindoo jurisprudence has a substratum of forethought and sound judgement, but irrational imitation has engrafted in it an immense apparatus of cruel absurdities."[31] (op.cit., p. 432)

3. "It must be stated in fairness to the great author (Maine) that at the time when he wrote his book, Oriental scholars were not aware of existence of *Arthsastra,* and Kautilya's *Arthasastra* had not seen the light of the day... the harsh language used by Maine about ancient Hindu lawyers must be characterised as wholly unjustified and based on insufficient knowledge of the development of Hindu law." (op.cit., p. 432)

---

30 *Early Law and Custom*, p.46.

31 Ancient Law, p.17

One does not know how Kautilya's *Arthasastra* could remain suppressed for so long and why it still is not being given proper recognition. The sum total is that over a passage of time, the high pedestal accorded to our woman was lowered down both in reality as well as in perception. The worst disservice to women was done by the later writers of law, after the early centuries of Christian era, who framed such rules like the prohibition of widow remarriage in the *Kaliyug* as a *kali-varjya-vidhi* [32] and even demanded from eleventh century onwards that the widows tonsure i.e. shave off their head. The social organisation became decadent, when rules and ordinances, sanctions and prohitions came to be enforced without enquiry about the spirit of the law and sometimes in violation of it. To top it all, every distortion was eulogised as sanctioned by Manu whose works basically continue to govern the Hindu male psychology even now. When divergent opinions were expressed by Manu himself the ones curtailing woman's rights were kept in mind. Though the *Nirukta* of Yaksa (c.700 B.C.) quotes a verse mentioning Manu on the right of both sons and daughters to inheritance [33] but such texts were conveniently forgotten. While we associate Laxmi, the Goddess of wealth and prosperity with every housewife, giving the latter the satisfaction of being called a *grah Laxmi* (household controller) in actuality another edict of Manu has been made to override his other dictums till even today by which, "In childhood a female must be subject to her father, in youth to her husband, when her Lord is dead to her sons. A woman must never be independent." [34]

---

[32] H.C. Chakladar, *Some Aspects of Social Life in Ancient India, The Cultural Heritage of India*, op.cit., vol. ii, p.579. For a fuller treatment of the prohibition in later times, see Batuknath Bhattacharya, *Kalivarjyas*, Calcutta, 1943.

[33] Manu III. 3; V. Raghavan, op.cit., *The Cultural Heritage of India*, vol. ii., p. 335.

[34] Manu II, 145.

Strict control has, however, had its own ramifications. From her birth, the girl is treated by the father as a burden, to be got rid off by marriage at the earliest opportunity. From her childhood she is trained to look after her future unknown husband who, except for earning a livelihood neglects all duties at home and expects his wife, even when she is earning herself, to look after him as a lord and master. The *grah Laxmi* in most cases is reduced to be a menial servant; the *devi* (goddess) becoming a *dasi* (slave). She in her turn, pampers her son much to the discomfiture of her own daughter. Later, these two females take it back on the daughter-in-law. Fortunately, today's educated girl does not want any inferiority complex to mar her growth and prefers to live alone with her husband. She also deplores that while we worship Mother Saraswati as goddess of learning, we deny our young damsels the right of learning. The high percentage of forced fallout of our girls even from primary schools brings out our criminal neglect in this field. Are we then not merely paying lip service to the image of Saraswati? It is, however, heartening to note that in their sublime manner the girls are beginning to voice their innate feelings. Recently in Calcutta, where Saraswati *puja* (worship) is carried out on a mass scale on a fixed date, young girls affixed a placard below each one of her hundreds of idols which asked Mother Saraswati as to why her daughters were being denied the right of learning. Is it not for us to answer this question? Is not a fresh look, a change in our attitude, required? What is it after all that our women are demanding? None of them wants a status superior to man. All they are asking for is equal position, that is equal access to new opportunities, equality of treatment and equality of results. Would Saraswati, or we, deny it to them ?

When we were slaves, as we shall see later, we had hardly any option except to keep our women back. On attaining our freedom after a long struggle in which our women played a distinguished role, man and woman earnestly hoped that the new dawn would clear up the skies. Has it? The condition of our women has worsened after 40 years of independence as if this landmark was achieved only by and for our men. The contrast between the moral tone of ancient India, whatever it was, and the social pattern of modern India is sufficient to disprove the theory of evolution upwards. Women-power will, no doubt, show up. It is inborn in their heritage. The transformation of Parvati to *Durga, Kali* and *Shakti* (Divine Power) had not been too much of a time consuming process. Brahma, Vishnu and Siva still remain confined to their roles as Creator, Protector and Destroyer. Mother *Shakti*, when the need arose, assumed all the three powers in her ownself to combat and destroy the evil. Now that devilry is crossing all limits, would Mother Parvati not take up the cudgels again as *Shakti* to destroy the demon even if she has to become so uncontrollable that it would need all the powers of Vishnu to destroy her ? Is that our aim ?

We should also have the courage to take a correct perspective of actions of the most graceful Mother Sita. She had to go through the worst known form of subjugation for 14 years, yet she came out bright. When she was made to go through the fire test, why was no objection put up by Lord Hanuman, the symbol of unlimited power, who had personally witnessed her agony and in defiance of her suffering single-handed burnt down the capital of Lanka in contempt? And why did Prince Lakshman, who was a witness to the melodrama of the fire test, alongwith a thousand victors, agree to confine her to the forest on the wayward doubts of a single subject even when she was pregnant? In all her graciousness she accepted the ordeal again. Today some are distorting the great epic to such an extent that there was a widespread feeling calling for her ouster and she voluntarily demanded her solitary exile not in atonement of any folly but to restore the honour of King Rama. And the wise men of today, on seeing this gross falsification tend to ignore the distortion feeling exalted that it will save our international image ! Underterred, Sita brought up her twin sons, who, on their own, successfully challenged her dear mighty husband without of course knowing the relationship. When, after armistice, Sita was beseeched to regain her rank as the Queen Consort, her soul rebelled so violently that its reverberations caused Mother Earth itself to burst out and soothen her by absorbing her within. But is that the end of the story? Does anyone ask why mother Sita chose mother Earth rather than rejoin her mighty *Chakravarti* Lord of the Universe? Was it not a rebuke , a rebuttal, at extreme cost, to remind us that woman was not a commodity to be thrown out and called in at man's mercy ?

Coming to Radha, the most worshipped lady around the universe, the world will remain cheerful by the fragrance of Platonic love, a true love that unites diverse beings to one another submerging them in a feeling that they belong to each other which develops them into higher beings. And some of us are getting inclined to reject this as an impractical concept.

One hopes that in time to come our scholars would devote some time to collect details pertaining to life of women in Europe and Africa before Christianity, in the Middle-East before Islam and in South Asia and the Far East before the advent of Hinduism and Buddhism there. In all probability this study will put a stop to the efforts that are being made by some to project our women's background in an inferior position compared to that of women in the corresponding period anywhere else. [35]

---

35 Some aspects have been excellently brought out in a small compilation of research work done by both men and women of different religions under the title, "*The Authority of the Religions and the Status of Women*", a Joint Women's Programme publication, 1989.

4

THE GOLDEN AGE AND ITS DECLINE

We may at this stage throw a coup d' oeil on developments of our contacts with the Western world and go back to the reign of Marcus Aurelius in Rome (A.D. 161-180). For this, let us take recourse to some excerpts from Augusts Toussaint's marvellous research.

"If it is necessary to characterise this period in the history of the Indian Ocean, the name 'golden age', given it by certain writers, seems still the most suitable. Perhaps 'age of gold' is even more appropriate, for the main element of the trade of the period was in fact that beautiful Roman gold coin, the aureus, the dollar of that day. Extraordinary quantities of this coin, according to Pliny, were despatched from Rome to India, as Rome had almost nothing else to offer the Indians in return for their products...

"What did Rome receive in return. If we consider only the articles mentioned in the Periplus, we could draw up an imposing list of products which then made up the substance of Eastern trade—nothing, however, similar to what today we call ' raw materials' but, on the contrary, almost uniquely luxury items: spices, perfumes, silks, muslins, tortoise-shell, ivory, pearls, precious stones, unguents, dyes, and other rare products..."[1]

Whatever the level, it involved going across the seas. The origin of Indian navigation has been carefully studied by Kennedy[2] which gives evidence of maritime trade in the sixth century B.C. between Bhakukacha (Broach) and Baveran (Babylon, Iraq).

---

[1] *Histoire De L' Océan Indian, Presses Universitaires de France*, 1961; *History of the Indian Ocean, London*, 1966.

[2] R.K. Mukherjee, *Indian Shipping*, Bombay, 1957, p.62.

Niveneh, the third capital of Assyria (Iraq) is also mentioned in the *Puranas* as Shonitpur, along with the race of the *Asuras* (Assyrians) and their King Asura Bana (Ashur-banipal). Auguste Toussaint brings out :-

"That Indian merchants had been in Egypt and even as far as Rome during the Hellenistic and Roman periods is also well established but their number was infenitesimal compared to the foreign merchants who at that time frequently visited the ports of India. India has every reason to be thankful since she had no need to launch out on the conquest of distant Americas to obtain a supply of metallic currency and she thus escaped the vicissitudes of the exploiting people who were forced to go out and seek their fortune far from their own lands.

"But although she was not a conquering maritime power she nonetheless moved into the countries of the Indian Ocean. In fact, long before she was colonised herself, she gave proof of a very remarkable colonising activity, which long remained unknown until a French orientalist, Coedés, revealed it to the world, a short time back, in a work [3] which none of those interested in oceanic hitory should fail to read.

" A 'colonising activity', we have called it, but we must add that the word 'colonising' is not meant in the popular sense; or perhaps we should say that, on the contrary, it was true colonisation. Is not peaceful penetration , both economic and cultural, and occurring with the full consent of those colonised, for whom it proves beneficial and lasting in its effects, is not this, in fact, real colonisation?" [4]

---

[3] G. Coedés, *Les États hindouisés d'Indochine et d'Indonésie*, Paris, 1948. (Hinduised States of Indo-China and Indonesia).

[4] Toussaint, op. cit., p.61.

According to Coédes, the geographical area involved in this Indian colonisation included the region called in French, Insulinde, the Malay Archipelago (exclusive of the Phillipines) and Indochina along-with the Malay Peninsula and Burma. The English writer, Hall, traces relations between India and these regions to pre-history and stresses that interchange of people used to take place at a very early time. Gradual infiltration and consolidation lasted from the first to the sixth centuries, and the second, one of development and ever-increasing fruition, from the seventh to the tenth centuries.

Van Leur maintains it is highly improbable that the agents of colonisation of Greater India were tradesmen and sailors. In his opinion, the planting of the Indian culture in the Malaya Archipelago was due to the initiative of the Indonesian ruling classes who called the Indian priesthood eastwards. Alongside the priesthood, Indian artifice came to the royal courts. Toussaint adds:

"The religious regulation forbidding orthodiox Hindus to associate with foreigners was not respected in the circumstances, for we have testimony showing that the Brahmin immigrants married the natives. The Indian influence expressed itself in a transformation of local customs in the form of institutions and works which have survived the erosion of time... The temples in Angkor in Cambodia and Borobudur in Java are among the most famous of these."[5]

"Some historians (Hall, Harrison etc.) point out that Buddhism played a most important part in this cultural phenomenon and it even survived Hinduism in most of the regions concerned. The astonishing part is that although originally Buddhism was propagated in China by the Indians, eventually it was the Chinese who went out in search of it in India. The Chinese Buddhist voyage between the fourth and tenth centuries should be seen

---

[5] Toussaint, op. cit., p.64.

against the background of this quest, unique in the history of religion." [6]

Another development also contributed to the downfall of Hindudom in Greater India. In the ninth century, according to the Arab historian, Baladhuri, there were, if not real colonies, at least notable settlements of Muslim merchants on the Malabar Coast and in several cities on the sea coast as far north as the Indus.

At about the same period, trade links were established between the countries of the Western Mediterranean, India and China, initiated by the Jewish merchants. The Arab geographer Ibn Khurdadhbih (c.850) wrote: "These merchants speak Persian, Roman (Greek and Latin), Arabic and the Frankish, Spanish, and Slav languages. They travel from West to East and from East to West, sometimes by land, sometimes by sea. From the West they bring back eunuchs, female slaves, boys, silk, furs and spices... On their return they load up with musk, aloes, camphor, cinnamon and other products of the Eastern countries..."[7]

By the thirteenth century a large Muslim colony was established by the traders at Perlak, in northern Sumatra. The entire Malay Archipelago was then under the dominion of the kingdom of Madjapahit, and the propagation of Islam was effective in gradually alienating the leaders of the coastal regions from their allegiance to that kingdom. Later, the opposition to the Portugese, after they had taken Malacca in 1511, reinforced Islam's position in that region. On this point, Toussaint says, "Van Leur also points out that the

---

[6] Toussaint, op. cit., p.81.

[7] From the curious collection of Ibn Shahriyar entitled *Ajaib al Hind*, or *The Wonders of India*, which dates back to about 960. Translated into French by M. Devic and published in 1878 as *Les Merveilles de l'Inde*. There is an English translation by P. Quennel (1926) and a new French translation by Sauvaget in *Mémorial Jean Sauvaget*, Damascus, 1954; Toussaint op.cit., p.49.

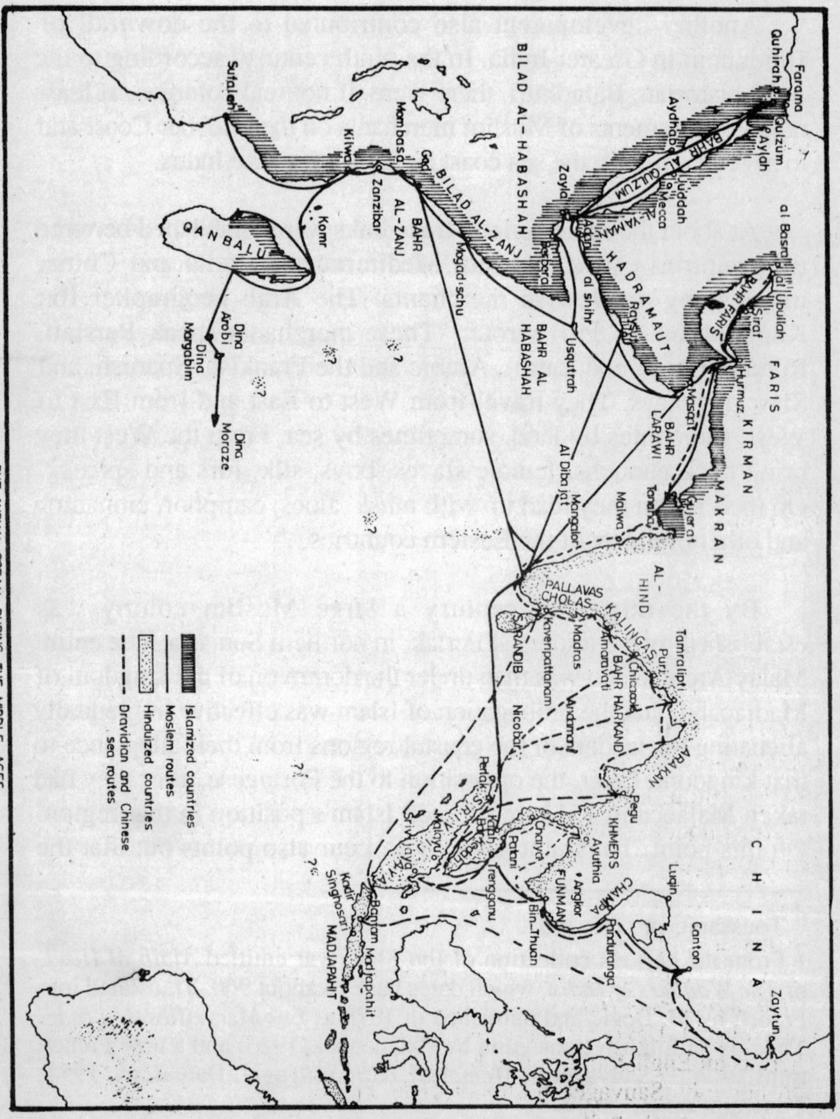

THE INDIAN OCEAN DURING THE MIDDLE AGES

propagation of Islam in the Malay Archipelago was by no means cultural in nature , for its agents were not learned men but simple merchants with little education. Also, Islam brought no new economic system to Indonesia. Besides, as we shall see further on, Chinese influence remained predominant in commercial matters in that region even after its Islamisation. Nor was customary law much influenced by Koranic Law". [8] He queries :

"To what conclusion, then, can we come ? The study of the history of Greater India has only just begun... The remarkable civilisation of Greater India is the result not of one sole factor but of several, about which generations and generations of scholars will wrangle *ad infinitum*" [9] On this question sociologist Quaritch Wales explicitly states his idea on the reciprocal contribution of the Indian and the native elements. [10] As a consequence, the exit of Hinduism from most parts of Greater India did not leave behind any trace of remorse or rancour.

---

8 Toussaint, op. cit., p.69.
9 Toussaint, op. cit., p.67.
10 *Pre-history and Religion in South-East Asia*, London, 1957.

5

THE EXOTIC FIELDS

Victory gained in distant lands or across ethnic or linguistic bonds, unless achieved through peaceful penetration, has always added prized laurels to chauvinistic jingoism. Power exercised by a few of one clan over a large number of the other has always remained a source of pride even after age and times have reduced the former to be mere skeletons of their earlier selves. In most cases alien women have been the most prized objects. In this struggle to establish one's superiority we find that many times one woman has been the cause of repeated assaults or subsequent armistice. Ingenuity of the male from time to time has reduced or elevated her to be the cause of national destruction, shame, redemption or honour. One wedlock by Chandragupta Maurya with the daughter of defeated Nictor Séleucos I, who founded the Greek dynasty in India in 312 BC, not only obliterated all the glory that Alexander the Great achieved earlier but got him (Maurya) the great satrapies covered by Herat, Kandahar, Kabul and Makran. Napolean tried to cement the empire in 1809 when he married Princess Marie Louise, the 18-year-old daughter of the Austrian emperor, just as his éclat forced the Polish hierarchy to persuade countess Marie Walewska to surrender. Much recently, in 1971, the wretched Yahya Khan of Pakistan made the vain effort to get the mass backing of his demoralised soldiers, when he encouraged them to plant a Pakistani flag in every Bangladeshi womb. Such has been the arduous course taken by history that sexual ardour provided the aphrodisiac to national vanity. Such has been the path shown by the heroes of yore that even today religious bigots feel elated, whenever the male member of one of their clan brings in a female unbeliever within the fold.

It is an irony that sometimes injured vanity, in quest for quick reprisal, blinded one's judgment and people got submerged in inevitable disaster by a disgruntled individual's throwing invitations to hungry hordes waiting on the sidelines who gladly seized the opportunity. As we go through some of earlier conquests, we find it was not charitable aid but desire for alien *zar, joru aur zamin* (wealth, women and land) which provided inspiration to the spirit that marched forward to fresher fields.

6

THE RISE OF THE CRESCENT

In the ninety fifth year of the *Hegira*, (*Samwat* 769, A.D. 713), Mohamed Bin Kasim, the general of the Caliph Walid of Iraq entered Sind. Having been invited by the Buddhist monks, when the local lowly Jats were most dissatisfied and in revolt, it was for the first time that the arms of Islam crossed the Indus.

It is the sad end of Kasim that has brought him in the format of this narration. If there is nothing more ferocious than a wounded tigress, there is nothing more voracious than the spirit of vengeance which drives women to machinate plots more harmful in intensity than any crafty Machiavellian can divine.

In 718 A.D. Mohamed Bin Kasim vanquished Dahir, prince of Sind, after numerous conflicts. He had spent much time and thought to construct bridges to cross the rivers and had sharp spikes put around his assault boats that pierced through the opponent's boats. When told before a major battle that the flag on the forty–yards–high temple inside the fort had a talisman tied around, on which the Hindus had great faith, he ordered from Iraq munjaneekas or ballistas with reach enough to blast the temple's dome as well as explosives to breach the walls, the former being the first target. "It is a surprise that the Buddhists submitted to wholesale conversion, whereas the Hindus survived this onslaught and preserved their ancestral faith, in spite of the persecutions for recalcitrance or offer of blandishments as the price of apostasy." [1]

Among the spoils of victory sent to the Caliph on this occasion were the daughters of the subjugated monarch who became the cause of Kasim's miserable end. "The two young princesses, in

---

1 Satkar Mookerjee, *Budhism in Indian Life and Thought, The Cultural Heritage of India*, op.cit., vol. i, p. 596.

order to revenge the death of their father, represented falsely to the Caliph that Mohamed Kasim had been connected with them. The Caliph, in a rage, gave order for Mohamed Kasim to be sewed up in a raw hide, and sent in that condition to court. When the mandate arrived at Tatta, Kasim was prepared to carry an expedition against Harchand, monarch of Kanouj. When he arrived at court, the Caliph showed him to the daughters of Dahir, who expressed their joy upon beholding their father's murderer in such a condition".[2]

And now let us see another end which beckoned the Great Bappa who, at 15, was the favourite vassal of the Mori Prince of Mewar, his uncle. When the foreign foe appeared, Bappa undertook the conduct of war. Victory smiled on him.

The foe retreated and was pursued by Bappa. Selim, who held Cambay, was attacked and forced to surrender. Bappa, contrary to his religion, married the daughter of the conquered Selim. Thereafter, Bappa took Cheetore from the Mori and became the *Mor* (Crown) of the land, and 'Sun of the Hindus' (*Hindu Sooraj*). His Hindu children rose to 98 in number.

The close of Bappa's carrer in Mewar is the strangest part of the legend. They say, *dans chaque crime, cherchez la femme* (in every crime, look for the woman). Selim's daughter seems to have mesmerised the thriving Bappa and Tod says, "We have a right to infer that it was from the influence acquired by this union, that he ultimately abandoned the sovereignty of Mewar and the title of *Hindu Sooraj*, to beome the founder of the 'one hundred and thirty tribes of *Nosherya Pathan's* of the west." [3] He left for Iran in AD 764, when the diadem of sovereignty was torn from the brow of the Hindu to adore that of Tatar. "Advanced in years, he abandoned his children and his counry, carried his arms West to Khorassan, and there established himself, and married new wives

[2] *Ayeen Akbery* vol. ii, p. 119; Tod, op.cit., vol. i, p. 199.

[3] Tod, op.cit., vol. i, p.202.

from among the 'barbarians' by whom he had a numerous offspring. Bappa reached the partriarchal age of one hundred years when he died ... after having overcome all the kings of the west, as in Ispahan, Kandahar, Cashmere, Irak, Iran, Tooran and Cafferist'han; all of whole daughters he married, and by whom he had one hundred and thirty sons called the Nosherya Pathans. Each of them founded a tribe bearing the name of the mother... the chronicles also record that the the subjects of Bappa quarelled for the disposal of his remains. The Hindu wished the fire to consume them; the 'barbarian' to commit them to earth; but on raising the pall while the conflict was raging, innumerable flowers of the lotus were found in the place of the remains of mortality: these were conveyed and planted on the lake..." [4]

It was in 986 A.D. that the Amir of Ghazni, Sabuktigin, made a significant raid in Punjab and carried with him a large booty. In 997 A.D. he was succeeded by his son Mahmood who made twelve invasions. Though these annual attacks were always repulsed, the atrocities committed on Indian women during these regular assaults left deep indelible marks on the Indian psyche which only a long passage of time could have eroded. But in less than two hundred years another invitation was thrown out which proved to be disastrous. How one woman could change the face of history or destiny of a people, Sanyogta, the daughter of Jeychand, the king of Canouj, perhaps could never visualise. Her admiration for Prithvi Raj Chohan, the king of Delhi, may have guided her to garland the latter's statue put by her own father at her *syamvar* and then allow her to be lifted out of the regal assembly by the hidden Prithvi Raj on his charger. Alone this would have gone down as a great relic of Cupid's arrow. However, the short-sighted Jeychand's treacherous invitation to Muhammad Ghori to avenge his own domestic disgrace brought worse havoc than what even Mahmood Ghazni could conceive of.

---

[4] Tod, op.cit., vol. i, p.186.

The combined power of Ghori and Jeychand was humiliated by Prithvi Raj in 1191 A.D. Captured Ghori was pardoned and let loose on oath never to return. Ghori decided to settle the score again, notwithstanding the oath. Women are the embellishments of power; their pursuit can also be the biggest hinderence in attaining it. According to Ferishta, Muhammad Ghori spoke at the time of his undertaking the second onslaught :-

"Ever since I have been defeated by the princes of Hind, I have kept myself aloof from any contact with a woman. I have not changed my clothes and for a whole year in sorrow, regret and dejection I have not allowed the Amirs of... who having run away from the battle were presenting themselves to me... Now in faith of the greatness of God I advance towards Hind."

During this time Prithvi Raj allowed himself to be submerged in Sanyogtas and wine with obvious results. After the assassination of Muhammad Ghori by a blinded, captured Prithvi Raj's arrow, Qutb-ud-din Aibak, a Turkoman slave, rose to become the first Sultan of Delhi. He. was succeeded by another Turkish general Altamash (1211-36). His daughter, Sultana Raziyah-ud-din (1236-40) succeeded him and married a Turkish chief in the hope that he would be able to assist her but she was no match for the jealous band of Turkish chiefs known as 'the forty', who, moreover, hated being ruled over by a woman. After her murder, a period of further anarchy followed.

7

HOLOCAUST

Later, Ala-ud-din of the Khilji tribe came on the scene. In 1296, he returned after his notorious invasion of the Deccan laden with booty. The old king Jalal-ud-din Khilji, his uncle, went out to welcome his victorious nephew and while he was clasping his hand, Ala-ud-din basely had him murdered by one of his followers. Ala-ud-din advanced upon Delhi with his uncle's head held aloft upon a lance. He then conducted a campaign against the Rajput fortress of Cheetore where at that time a young prince Lukumsi was on the throne.

Bheemsi was the uncle of the young prince, and protector during his minority. He had espoused the daughter of Hamir Sank (Chohan) of Ceylon. Her name was Pudmani, a title bestowed only on the superlatively fair. Having failed in the first attempt, Ala-ud-din mustered his strength and attacked again. When success deluded him, he limited his demand to the possession of Pudmani. At length he restricted his desire to a mere sight of this extraordinary beauty, finally reducing it to the proposal of beholding her through the medium of mirrors which was accepted. Relying on the faith of the Rajpoot, he entered Cheetore slightly guarded, and having gratified his wish, returned. Bheemsi, unwilling to be outdone in confidence, accompanied the king to the foot of the fortress. Here Ala-ud-din had an ambush; Bheemsi was made prisoner, hurried away to the Tatar camp, and his liberty made dependent on the surrender of Pudmani. Despair reigned in Cheetore when this fatal event was known, and it was debated whether Pudmani should be resigned as a ransom for Bheemsi. When she was informed of this, she expressed her acquiescence and equipped herself with wherewithal to secure her from dishonour. Two chiefs of her own kin and clan of Ceylon, her uncle Gorah, and his nephew Badal, however devised a scheme for the liberation of their prince without hazarding her life or fame. Intimation was despatched to Ala-ud-din that on the day he withdrew from his trenches the fair Pudmani would be sent, surrounded by her females and handmaids, not only those who would accompany her to Delhi, but many others who desired to pay her their last mark of reverence. Seven hundred covered litters proceeded to the royal camp. In each was placed one of the bravest of the defenders of Cheetore, borne by six armed soliders disguised as litter-porters. When they reached the camp, half an hour was granted for a parting interview between the Hindu prince and his bride. They then placed their prince in a litter and some returned with him. After some time the devoted band issued from their litters; but Ala-ud-din was too well guarded. Pursuit was ordered and those who guarded the return of the prince perished to a man. A fleet horse had been kept in reserve for Bheemsi, but at the outer gate of the fort the host of Ala-ud-din was encountered. The choicest of the heroes of Cheetore met the assault. Bheemsi succeeded in ascending the fort and for a time Ala-ud-din was defeated in his object.

Ala-ud-din returned in 1303 A.D. Siege was laid and when eleven of his twelve sons had fallen in turn, Bheemsi called his chiefs around him and said, "Now I devote myself for Cheetore." "But another awful sacrifice was to precede this act of self-devotion in that horrible rite, the *Johur*, where females are immolated to preserve them from pollution or captivity. The funeral pyre was lighted within the 'great subterranean retreat', in chambers impervious to the light of day, and the defenders of Cheetore beheld in procession the queens, their own wives and daughters, to the number of several thousands. The fair Pudmani closed the throng, which was augmented by whatever of female beauty or youth could be tainted by Tatar lust. They were conveyed to the cavern, and the opening closed upon them, leaving them to find security from dishonour in the devouring element. A contest now arose between the Rana and his surviving son; but the father prevailed, and Ajeysi, in obedience to his commands, with a small band passed through the enemy's lines... The Rana, satisfied that his line was not extinct now prepared to follow his brave sons; and calling around him his devoted clans, for whom life had no longer any charms, they threw open the portals and descended to the plains and with a reckless despair carried death, or met it, in the crowded ranks of Alla. The Tatar conqueror took possession of an inanimate capital, strewed with brave defenders the smoke yet issuing from the recesses where lay consumed the once fair object of his desire".[1]

Ala-ud-din was followed by a number of sultans when the country was brought to the verge of total disaster. In 1451, Bahlol Lodi, an Afghan took Delhi "with the help of Jasrath Khokar, the ruler of N.W. Punjab."[2] In the strife-torn period at the beginning of the sixteenth century, Zahir-ud-din Muhammed, nicknamed Babar, appeared in Central Asia. In 1504, he quitted Samarkand and settled in Kabul as a fugitive. In 1524, a quarrel broke out between Sultan Ibrahim Lodi of Delhi, the grandson of Bahlol, and his nobles and Babar received an invitation from Alam Khan, the Sultan's uncle. Babar, nothing loath, accepted the invitation. He marched to Panipat to measure his sword with Ibrahim. Fortune returned to his standard. Thereafter an empire was created—so grand in its majesty—that the most picturesque peacock had to be recreated in the choicest and most precious diamonds, rubies and emeralds to provide a worthy throne for one of his descendants at a cost then of one crore rupees.[3]

---

[1] Tod, op.cit., vol.i, p. 215.

[2] J.C. Narang, *Regional Structure of India in Relation to Language and History; The Cultural Heritage of India,* op.cit., vol. i, p. 51.

[3] Rawlinson, op.cit., p. 202.

8

CONQUEST AND CONSOLIDATION BY THE GRAND MOGHULS

In A.D. 1528 Babar advanced from Agra to oppose Rana Sanga of Cheetore. Babar was the first who introduced field guns in India and this volcano of the field, this 'God of War' , played dreadful havoc in the close ranks of Rajpoot cavalry who kept on charging regardless. When the battle was still doubtful, Babar determined to renounce his besetting sun, destroyed the wine flasks and made his followers swear on the Quran to conquer or perish. The naïveté of his vow must be given in his own words:-

"I had always resolved, one time or another, to make an effectual repentance... I said to myself, 'O, my soul',

"How long will thou continue to take pleasure in sin?
Repentance is not unpalatable - taste it." (Persian verse).

"At this time... a general consternation and alarm prevailed among great and small. There was not a single person who uttered a manly word, nor an individual who delivered a courageous opinion... I called an assembly of all the *Amris* and officers, and addressed them.

"The most high God has now placed us in such a crisis, that if we fall in the field we die the death of martyrs; if we survive, we rise victorious, the avengers of the cause of God. Let us then, with one accord, swear on God's holy word, that none of us will even think of turning his face from this warfare, nor desert from the battle and slaughter that ensues, till his soul is separated from his body..."[1]

Little did the Rajpoots know of the vows being taken on the 'other side of the hill'. Suffice it to say that self-abanegation did infuse a singularity in the maintenance of Babar's aim. Sanga

---

[1] *Memoirs of Babar*, pp. 354-357; Tod, op. cit., vol. i, p.243.

retreated towards the hills of Mewar, having announced his fixed determination never to re-enter Cheetore but with victory. Had his life been spared to his country, he might have redeemed the pledge; but the year of his defeat was the last of his existence.

Tod adds, "Polygamy is the fertile source of evil, moral as well as physical, in the east... The desire of each wife, that her offspring should wear a crown, is natural ... and the love of power too often furnishes instruments for any deed, however base. When we see, shortly after the death of Sanga, the mother of his second son intriguing with Babar... to supplant the lawful heir, we can easily suppose she would not have scrupled to remove any other bar... That Babar respected and dreaded his foe we have the best proof, in his not risking another battle with him; and the blame which he bestows on himself for the slackness of his pursuit after victory is honourable to Sanga... when he says, Rana Sanga attained his present high eminence by his own valour and his sword".[2]

Babar may have prayed to cleanse himself from all his sins but till his very end he remained enraptured and obsessed by his favourite object, a youthful male. This passion for unisexual unison, despite victory, perhaps delayed establishment of the Moghul harems. However, to strengthen his conquest, Babar went to the extreme extent of praying to Allah to give his own life to Humayun, his ailing son.

Humayun proved himself a true knight throughout the tumultuous period that he had to go through. Karnavati, the mother of the infant prince Odai Sing — son of Rana Sanga against whom Babar had fought — had taken a pledge of protection from him when she sent a *rakhi,* an offer of sisterhood, to this monarach which was accepted. Later, Cheetore, the palladium of Hinduism, was besieged by muslim sultans of Central India. Humayun, on receiving a message demanding fulfilment of the solemn pledge given by him, abandoned his conquests in Bengal and moved back

---

[2] Tod, op.cit., vol. i, p.246

to redeem his pledge and to succour Cheetore but arrived too late to prevent the recurrence of a *johar* or save his sister. Karnavati led the procession of willing victims to their doom and thirteen thousand females were thus swept at once from the record of life.

It is interesting to note how power failed to incite the bug that should have tickled the passion for lady love in Humayun. He was engrossed in initial battles against followers of his own faith, whose ethnic and lingual dissimilarity remained a hurdle against unity under any common banner. Fortunes fluctuated, victory smiling alternately on one group or the other of the invaders. Neither the victor nor the vanquished however had any women to offer as a ransom that could forge a common platform. But having settled their scores, there was no need to have their own women when there was so much scope in the real *jannat, Hind* itself, which later dynasts continued to acclaim,

"If on earth be an Eden of bliss,
It is this, it is this, nothing but this."[3]

One man who really earned his entry into this heaven, paying a price for it at each step to ensure he got his reward in this life itself, was Akbar. Little did Humayun know that his son Akbar's ambitious thrist of conquest would result in another *johar* being commanded at Cheetore itself. When flames had provided sanctuary to their womenfolk against all possible satanic overtures, 8,000 Rajpoots ate the last *beera* together, put on their sattron robes and none survived to stain the 'yellow mantle' by inglorious surrender.

In 1567, Pratap succeeded to the titles and renown of the illustrious house of Cheetor when Odai Sing left it but without a capital, without resources, his kindred and clans disspirited by reverses. Only two years subsequent to Pratap's succession, Rao Maldeo of Mundore was enticed by Akbar to follow the example

---

[3] Rawlinson, op.cit., p. 202.

set by Raja Bhagwan Das of Amber (Jaipur) and place himself at his footstool. The Rao sent his son Oodi—*le gros*—to pay homage to Akbar. Oodi was the first prince to give his daughter in marriage to Akbar. The bribe for which the Rao bartered his honour was enormous. Four provinces, yielding £ 200,000 of annual revenue, were given in exchange of Joda Bae, at once doubling his fisc. [4] The Rao was made Raja of Marwar and the descendant of the king of Canouj gained the 'right hand' of the emperor of the Moghuls. Soon Bhagwan Das of Jaipur also gave his sister to the Moghul. When Hindu pride and prejudice were thus violated by some princes in Rajasthan, the Rana renounced all alliances with those who were so degraded. Without offering any defence to cover the eternal shame left behind by those princes who auctioned their nobility, one may at least say that their inner-most self could never live down the sense of guilt they went through. When Pratap expressed his regret to eat with Bhagwan Das' son, Raja Man Singh of Amber, the Commander-in-Chief of the Moghul Forces, as, "He could not eat with a Rajpoot who gave his sister to a Toork and who probably ate with him", Raja Man Singh withdrew, observing, "It was for the preservation of your honour that we sacrificed our own and gave our sisters and daughters to the Toork; but abide in peril, if such be your resolve, for this country shall not hold you"; and mounting of his visit affirmed, "If I do not humble your pride, my name is not Man"; to which Pratap replied, "He should be always happy to meet him"; while someone, in less dignified terms, desired he would not forget to bring his *Phoopa* (uncle) Akbar.

Bundi was an early object of Akbar's attention and he besieged it in person. He had been some time before its impregnable walls, without the hope of its surrender. Raja Man decided to use his influenc to make the Prince of Bundi faithless to his pledge to hold the castle as a fief of Cheetore. By courtesy, never laid aside among belligerent Rajpoots, he obtained access to the castle and the emperor accompanied him in the guise of a mace-bearer. Akbar was soon recognisied. A treaty was drawn up upon the spot,

---

[4] Tod, op.cit., vol. i, p.267.

Raja Man willingly suffered the twin humiliations of having to accept the prefix of being a disgrace to his class as well as being denied command over one brought down by his caprice. The mighty emperor was also denied the privilege to have a woman of this State either on a permanent basis or as a one time pleasure.

The text of treaty :-

"1. That the Chief of Boondi should be exempted from that custom, degrading to a Rajpoot, of sending a *dola* to the royal harem (*Dola* is the term for a princess affianced to the King).
2. Exemption from the *Jezya*, a poll tax.
3. That the chiefs of Boondi should not be compelled to cross the Attoc.
4. That the vassals of Boondi should be exempted from the obligation of sending their wives or female relatives to hold a stall in the *Meena bazar*, at the palace on the festival of *Noroza*.
5. That they should have the privilege of entering the *Dewane-aum*, or 'hall of audience', completely armed.
6. That their sacred edifices should be respected.
7. That they should never be placed under the command of a Hindu leader.
8. That their horses should not be branded with the imperial *dagh* (This brand *dagh* was a flower on the forehead)... "[5]

With undaunted heroism and inflexible determination, Pratap persevered alone to keep honour bright. But even he, whose fortitude had remained unsubdued when he was beset on every side, dislodged from the most secret retreats, hunted from glen to glen, was shaken by a piercing cry from his daughter when a wild cat darted on the reserved portion of her food. The agony of hunger made her shrieks insupportable and 'unmanned' the tiger for the time being. It was only Prithi Raj, a nobleman of his own entourage, who had earlier been compelled to follow the car of

---

[5] Tod, op.cit., vol. ii, p.383.

Akbar, who saved the day. When the overjoyed Akbar exultingly showed him Pratap's letter asking for mitigation of his hardships, he affirmed that the letter was forgery and in a secret message remonstrated to Pratap not yield to Akbar, "the broker in the market of men," [6] and not to part with honour for *noroza*.

Noroza, the gaiety generated by Akbar to despoil that flower which earlier in a spirit of defiant self-preservation had preferred the path of self-immolation to be burnt alive in *johars*, rather than suffer the dishonour of being trampled under the feet of the barbarian! Akbar had a different woman every night except for Joda Bae. For deep sea angling he took recourse to the *purdah* of his own queen. Abul Fazil clarifies, "It (*Noroza*) is not New Year's Day, but a festival especially instituted by Akbar... held on the ninth day (*no-roza*) following the chief festival of each month... The queen also had her court, when the wives of the nobles and the Rajpoot vassal princess were congregated... His Majesty is also there in disguise."[7] These 'ninth day fairs' were the markets in which Rajpoot honour was bartered. Prithi Raj was only preserved by the high courage and virtue of his wife, a princess of Mewar. Tod says, "On one of these celebrations of the *Khooshroz*, the monarch of the Moghuls was struck with the beauty of the daughter of Mewar, and he singled her out from amidst the united fair of *Hind* as the object of his passion. It is not improbable that an ungenerous feeling united with that already impure, to despoil the Seesodias of their honour, through a princess of their house under the protection of the sovereign. On retiring from the fair, she found herself entangled amidst the labyrinth of apartments by which egress was purposely ordained when Akbar stood before her: but insead of acquiescence, she drew a poniard from her corset, and held it to his breast, dictating, and making him repeat, the oath of renunciation of the infamy to all her race...[8]

It is time to return to the fortitude of Pratap who vowed 'to

---

6 Tod, op.cit., vol. i, p.273.

7 Abul Fazil, Tod, op.cit., vol. i, p.274.

8 Tod, op.cit., vol. i, p.275.

make his mother's milk resplendent'. Single-handed, for quarter of a century he withstood the combined efforts of the empire. He spurned every overture which had submission for its basis or called for the degradation of his race by uniting his family by marriage with the invader.

One solitary woman, one fair damsel from among the noble entourage, would have put an end to the endless misery of the great Pratap. Instead he kept the flame alive,

"... preferring

Hard liberty before the easy yoke
Of servile pomp."

One single woman would have put an end to all confrontation and also obliterated remnants of all national pride. Never then perhaps a Sivaji in down south Deccan, or a Guru Gobind Singh in the Punjab would have been inspired to take up cudgels from a scratch and inflame resurgence. Never perhaps a descendant, settled in Nepal, would have been able to hold on to his own both against the Moghuls and later the British.

Across the horrors of war, tributes could not be withheld from one whose valour so demanded. Khan Khanan, the first Moghul satrap (viceroy) of Delhi of Akbar paid his homage:

> "All is unstable in this world: land and wealth will disappear, but the virtue of a great name lives forever. Putto (Pratap) abandoned wealth and land, but never bowed the head: alone of all the princes of *Hind*, he preserved the honour of his race". [9]

---

[9] Tod, op.cit., vol. i, p.272.

One cannot help making an observation here. Till today, there is not a single lane in Delhi named after Maharana Pratap whereas one of the best roads here is named after Man Singh. At the India Gate itself, where we kindle an *Amar Jyoti* in homage to our gallant soldiers, not a

In passing it would be of interest to note how the great Akbar bade farewell to his mighty empire. "A desire to be rid of the great Raja Man of Amber, to whom he was so much indebted, made the emperor descend to act the part of the assassin. He prepared a *majoom*, or confection, a part of which contained poison; but caught in his own snare he presented the innoxious portion to the Rajpoot and ate that drugged with death himself. We have a sufficient clue to the motives which influenced Akbar to a deed so unworthy of him... namely, a design on the part of Raja Man to alter the succession, and that Khoosru, his nephew, should succeed instead of Selim... the aged emperor... dared not openly undertake, without exposing the throne in his latter days to the dangers of civil contention , as Raja Man was too powerful to be openly assaulted." [10] . In 1605 Akbar died at Agra. "He was buried in a tomb he had built for himself at Sikandra. His funeral was a poor, hurried affair and, in 1691, the Jats who had risen in revolt, plundered the tomb and scattered the ashes. 'Thus does the world treat those from whom it expects no good and fears no evil'." [11]

Akbar was succeeded by Salim, the most charismatic Moghul ruler. His affair with Anarkali, the court dancer, would have gone down in the annals of amour as more sparkling than any had he allowed his royal ambitions to be buried together with her in the brick by brick entombment ordered for her by his father infuriated at the prospect of a court dancer being elevated to the rank of Joda Bae.

---

single name is inscribed of those who sacrificed their lives for the country after we won our independence. Nearby, the canopy that covered King George V's removed statue, has to be persevered with because our "intellectuals" proclaim it to be the relic of our "past art, culture and heritage" which we must preserve lest a loin-clothed Gandhi appears on the scene. If one dares to talk on such matters one would be called primitive!

[10] Tod, op.cit., vol. i, p.279.
[11] Rawlinson, op.cit., p. 188.

Salim ascended the throne under the title of Jahangir. He, in a way, unknowingly, contributed to the establishment of the British Empire in India. In 1608 the East India Company sent to Surat a fleet of merchant-ships, on board of which was Captain William Hawkins. Larry Collins and Dominique Lapierre have brought out how Hawkins achieved success when he set out from Surat: "Hawking marched off into the interior, prepared to find rubies as big as pigeons' eggs... potions derived from elephant's testicles to give him eternal youth. There was little of that India along the Captain's march to Agra. There, however, his encounter with the great Moghul compensated for the hardships of his journey. He found himself face to face with a sovereign beside whom Queen Elizabeth appeared the ruler of a provincial hamlet... The first Englishman to reach his court was greeted with a gesture which might have disconcerted the 125 worthy shareholders of the East India Trading Company. The Moghul made him a member of the Royal household and offered him as a welcoming gift the most beautiful girl in his harem, an Armenian Christian... Jehangir signed an imperial firman authorising the East India Company to open trading depots north of Bombay". [12]

Ambassador Galbraith adds, "A description survives of the daily routine of Jehangir, son of Akbar, written by an English companion, one Willam Hawkins. In the morning, after prayers, the emperor showed himself to the people at an oriel window in the palace. Having provided this reassurance he went to the women's apartments with such effect that he then rested there until three in the afternoon. Then he withnessed elephant fights or other sports and heard grievances and held court. Thereafter he went to his evening meal, for which he liked five kinds of meat, and then retired to his private apartments where he had five cups of wine, topped off with opium. This was in his active years; later on he drank and smoked [13] more and turned practical matters over to

---

12 *Freedom at Midnight*, Vikas, New Delhi, 1976, pp.10-11.

13 What he smoked has not been clarified. It was in Jahangir's reign that tobacco was introduced in India. (Tod, op.cit., vol. ii, p.507). The Portugese brought this evil into India in 1605 and Jahangir initially ordered its prohibition in 1617. (*Tuzuk-i-Jahangiri*, trans. by Rogers and

Nurjahan, the most talented of his wives."[14]

A word on Nurjahan, the brilliance of universe, whose captivating charm proved fatal to her first husband, Sherafghan, got killed by Jahangir out of jealousy in 1611. A most remarkable woman, she did succeed in making her presence felt, appearing with Jahangir in public at the *jharokha* or palace window and in the hunting field issuing *firmans*, and having her name impressed on the coinage. Her ruling passion was power, to obtain which she was quite unscrupulous. Jahangir was buried in the midst of a beautiful garden in Lahore, and a stately musoleum was erected over his remains. Close by sleeps his powerful and ambitious consort, in a simple tomb bearing the inscription,

> "Let neither lamp nor rose adorn my grave,
> To save a moth from courting death, or a nightingale the trouble of a song."[15]

Before she attained this sublime state, Nurjahan had to constantly exert against those who hated to see the empire being ruled by a woman. The Moghuls did not recognise primogeniture and the sons fought till the survivor succeeded to the throne. In the intrigues for succession, Nurjahan supported Prince Khurram, who was married to her brother Asaf Khan's daughter, Mumtaz Mahal. Earlier, the eldest prince Khusru was blinded and thrown into prison by Jahangir for rising in revolt against him. And Khurram to eliminate any threat, caused Khusru to be poisoned, assuming the title of Shah Jahan. On him, Galbraith says :-

---

edited by H. Beveridge, Royal Asiatic Society, London, vol. i, p. 374). But the decree seems to have remained a dead letter. Manucci, a traveller, mentions Rs.5000/- as tobacco duty realised for a day at Delhi alone. (Niccolao Venetian Manucci, *Storia do Mogor*, Eng. trans. by William Irvine, 1907-8) The Act was later abolished. (P.N. Chopra, *Some Experiments in Social Reforms in Mediaeval India; The Cultural Heritage of India*, op.cit., vol.ii p.634).

[14] John Kenneth Galbraith, *Ambassador's Journal*, Hamish Hamilton, London, 1969, p. 619.

[15] M.G. Rawlinson, op.cit., p.196.

"Shah Jahan, with Lorenzo, must be counted one of the two greatest art patrons of all time... He was a prodigious womaniser; each year there was an eight-day fair at his court at which the most attractive specimens from his dominions were displayed... In his late sixties he fell ill, one gathers from the carefully guarded comments of Bernier, a French physician then at the court, from an overdose of an aphrodisiac. His sons promptly began fighting and when he showed signs of getting well, he was deposed and locked up in Agra fort with a distant view of the Taj Mahal." [16] One must thank the Lord that Shah Jahan who gave Mumtaz Mahal 14 children to bear, got erected in her lasting memory the grand edifice of perfection, Taj Mahal, a tear on the cheek of eternity.[17] Fate and zealous fanaticism, however, combined together to put this grand monarch in secluded confinement. Jahangir was born of a Rajpoot princess and so was Shah Jahan. His crown prince, Dara Shikoh, also son of a Rajpoot queen, had too much of Hindu blood in his veins and he even translated into Persian ancient Hindu scriptures, the *Upanishads*, under the title of *Sirr-i-Akbar* (The Great Secret). In Annemarie Schimmel's words, it was a most remarkable work which became one of the 'sacred scriptures' of European idealist philosophers after Anquetil Duperron translated it into Latin in 1801. His younger brother, the ambitious Aurangzeb for his own selfish ends, whipped up religious frenzy and mobilished the bigots under his banner. Revenge first took the form of an attack on the Shias (the poets and scholars who had been coming in large numbers from Iran, and had assisted Akbar in his literary and religious experiments, were Shias). And the orthodox elements' final triumph came when Aurangzeb ascended throne after he had blinded and thrown into prison his brother, Dara Shikoh.

---

16 J.K. Galbraith, op.cit., pp. 620-21.

17 His annual revenue was stated to have been 22 crores of rupees. Taj Mahal cost four crores in 20 years. Rawlinson, op.cit., p. 202.

9

LIQUIDATION

In order to understand the complex personality of Aurangzeb, one should go through some extracts of his rebuke to his tutor Moola Salé given in an edition of Bernier (who was an eye witness at Moghul Court), printed in A.D. 1684, only three years after the event.

"What is it you would have of me, Doctor?... In the first place, you have taught me that all that *Frangistan* (so it seems they call Europe) was nothing, but I know not what little island, of which the greatest king was he of Protugal, and next to him he of Holland, and after him he of England: and as to the other kings; as those of France and Andalusia, you have represented them to me as our petty Rajas; telling me that the kings of *Indostan* were far above them all together and that they were the true and only Houmajons, the Ekbars, the Jehan-Guyres, the Chah-Jehans, the ones, the great ones, the conquerors and kings of the world; and that Persia and Usbec, Kachguer, Tatar and Catay, Pegu, China and Matchinadid tremble at the name of the kings of *Indostan*. Admirable geography! You should rather have taught me exactly to distinguish all those different states of the world, and well to understand their strength, their way of fighting, their customs, religions, governments and interests; and, by the perusal of solid history, to observe their rise, progress, decay, and whence, how, and by what accidents and errors those great changes and revolutions of empires and kingdoms have happened... Should not you, instead of your flattery, have taught me somewhat of that point so important to a king, which is, what the reciprocal duties are of a sovereign to his subjects and those of subjects to their sovereign; and ought not you to have considered, that one day I should be obliged with the sword to dispute my life and the crown with my brothers?... Have you ever taken any care to make me learn, what 'tis to besiege a town or to set an army in array? For these things I am obliged to others, not at all to you. Go and retire to the village whence you are come, and let no body know who you are or what is become of you."[1]

---

[1] Tod, op.cit. vol.i, pp. 298-299.

Rawlinson says, "In 1669 he issued a rescript to all the provincial governors to destroy with a willing hand the schools and temples of the infidels, and put an entire stop to the teaching and practice of idolatrous forms of worship. Temples were demolished all over the country and not even the sacred cities of of Benaras and Mathura were spared. Religious festivals and pilgrimages were stopped. The hated *jizya*, or poll-tax, which was regarded as a sign of national humiliation was revived. This policy had its inevitable results. There was widespread discontent, followed by rising all over the country." [2]

In 1654 Rana Raj Singh came on the throne of Cheetore. Tod brings out:

"An appeal to his gallantry made his throw down the gauntlet to Aurangzeb in the plentitude of his power... The Moghul demanded the hand of the princess of Roopnagurh, a junior branch of the Marwar house, and sent with the demand (a compliance with which was contemplated as certain) a cortege of two thousand horse to escort the fair to court. But the haughty Rajpootani... rejected with disdain the proferred alliance, and ... entrusted her cause to the arm of the chief of the Rajpoot race, offering herself as the reward of protection... the billet conveyed is incorporated in the memorial of this reign. 'Is the swan to be the mate of the stork: a Rajpootni, pure in blood, to be wife to the monkey-faced barbarian! ' concluding with a threat of self-destruction if not saved from dishonour. This appeal, with other powerful motives, was seized on with avidity by the Rana... With a chosen band he... cut up the imperial guards, and bore off the prize to his capital...

"The carrying off of his betrothed made Aurangzeb pour out all the phials of his wrath against Mewar... he denuded the very extremities of his empire to assemble a host which he deemed must prove irresistible. Akbar was recalled from his province, Bengal; Azim from the distant Cabul; and even Mauzum (the Mogul's heir)

---

2 Rawlinson, op.cit., p. 207.

from the war in the Dekhan. However, this formidable array supported by his guns, manned by Franks, *feringees* (Europeans), could not protect him against the just cause and avenging steel of the Rajpoot, and he was beaten and compelled to disgraceful flight, with an immense loss in men and equipment... [3]

A translation of the treaty of Mar, 1681, given below, throws some light on these unforgettable events.

++*Jowab Sawal* of Soor Singh and Nurhur Bhut (Uncle of Raja Raj Singh) with the Emperor

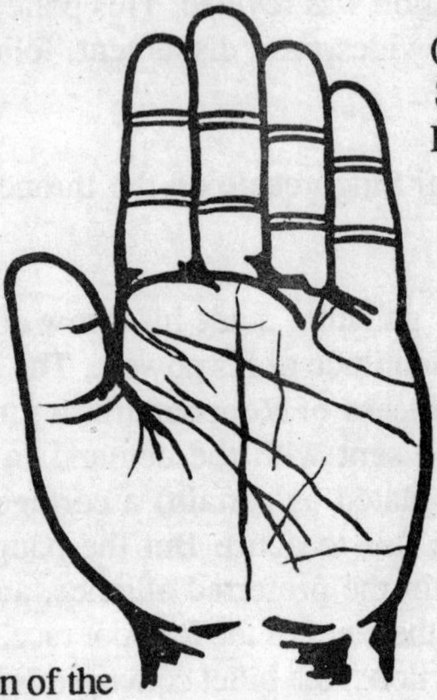

Punja or impression of the Emperor's hand with the word *Munzoori* written by himself

Munzoori (agreed)

++ Treaties or engagements are thus designated: literally stipulations and answers.

The treaty :

"1. Let Cheetore, with the districts adjacent appertaining thereto when it was inhabited, be restored.

"2. In such temples and places of Hindu religious resort as have been converted into mosques, the past cannot be

---

[3] Tod, op.cit., vol.i, pp. 301-306.

cannot be recalled, but let this practice be abolished.

"3. The aid hiherto afforded to the empire by the Rana shall be continued, but let no additional commands be imposed...[4]

Tod says, "Aurangzeb accumulated on his head more crimes than any prince who ever sat on an Asiatic throne". [5] Before passing this horrid stricture, he reflected, "Though myriads of victims who clung to their faith were sacrificed by him... yet nor these, nor the scrupulous fulfilment of fanatic observances, could soothe at the dread hour the perturbations of the 'still small voice' which whispered the names of father, brother, son, bereft by him of life. Eloquently does the portray says, 'Whichever way I look, I see only the divinity' — and that an offended divinity." [6] The agony is mirrored through the letters written to his sons a few days before his death in 1707.

"To Shaw Azim Shaw.

"Health to thee! my heart is near thee. Old age is arrived: weakness subdues me... The instant which passed in power hath left only sorrow behind it... My valuable time has been passed vainly. I had a patron in my own dwelling (conscience), but his glorious light was unseen by my dim sight... I brought nothing into this world, and except the infirmities of man, carry nothing out. I have a dread for my salvation, and with what torments I may be punished... regarding my acitions, fear will not quit me... The *Begum* (his daughter) appears afflicted; but God is the only judge of hearts. The foolish thoughts of women produce nothing but disappointment. Farewell! Farewell! Farewell!"

"To the Prince Kaum Buksh.

"My son, nearest to my heart... Now I depart a stranger, and

---

[4] Tod, op.cit., vol.i, pp. 309.

[5] Tod, op.cit., vol.i, pp. 309.

[6] Tod, op.cit., vol.i, pp. 300-301.

lament my own insignificance, what does it profit me? I carry with me the fruits of my sins and imperfections. Surprising Providence! I came here alone, and alone I depart... Wherever I look, I see nothing but the divinity... I have committed numerous crimes, and know not with what punishments I may be seized... Regard the *Begum* as without concern. *Odiporee,* your mother, was a partner in my illness, and wishes to accompany me in death; but every thing has its appointed time... No one has seen the departure of his soul; but I see that mine is departing."

They say what is in a name! On *Odiporee*, Tod opines, "Orme calls Kaum Buksh's mother a Cashmerian; certainly she was not a daughter of the Rana's family, though it is not impossible she may have been one of the great families of Shahpoora of Bunera (then acting independently of the Rana)..." [7] Enamoured of and infatuated with the idea of getting a Mewar princess how much vicarious satisfaction the Alamgir must have drawn to call her *Odiporee* is anyone's guess! [8]

Ultimately, ruin seized the ruthless King. "Aurangzeb's reign, which ended in 1707, marked the last phase of Moghul grandeur... The seizure of Delhi by Nadir Shah in 1739 was the final blow." [9] The Moghul power was extinct while the oppressed Rajpoots were again on the ascendant. What a downfall, the crumbling of a great empire due to sheer lunacy of a bigot. But this madness also produced other effects of a devastating nature. A stage came where no girl was to be found in affected areas. As to the extent to which female infanticide had reached in many parts of India we read in Lerchenfeld's work, "When in the year 1836 the first inquiry into this matter was made by the Anglo-Indian authorities, it was shown that , for example, in Western Rajputana in a group of 10,000 of

---

[7] Tod, op.cit., vol.i, pp. 301

[8] We do not know the fate of this *Odiporee*. Had she accompanied her lord perhaps a grand *sati mahal* would have been created in her honour for us to pay our obeisance to this *sati-mata* of ransom.

[9] Toussaint, op.cit., p. 151. The last Moghul, Bahadur Shah Zafar, was selected by the British to occupy the throne and the "Empire" extended no more than the boundary walls of Red Fort at Delhi.

the population there was not one girl! In Manikpur, the Rajpoot nobility admitted that in their district for more than 100 years no girl baby had lived longer than one year. A government official ascertained first the existence of the practice of murder in 308 districts which he had visited. In 26 he found not one girl under six years of age, in 28, not one under nubile age. In a few districts no marriage had taken place within the memory of man, and in one the last marriage dated 80 years back".[10]

Such an unparalleled self-inflicted ordeal, such a denial of the fair sex with all the comforts she bestows in her various froms, such submission to higher values that abnegated all that life can long for just for upholding one's women's personal honour, which people, where on earth, in which age, have undergone ?

The Moghuls no doubt made substantial contributions in the fields of art, crafts and architecture and did help create the music and everlasting symphony of different languages in the form of Urdu. However, during their rule there was a sudden fall in the dignified position occupied by Indian women. Education for women was stopped and they became victims of evil customs like very early child-marriage with attendant fallouts. The *purdah* system came to be established in this period even within the four walls of the joint family homes. Though in the field of property rights and right to divorce Muslim women were to some extent protected by their law but in practical application, due to the threat of instant divorce and little maintenance, the Indian Muslim women were made to go through such ordeals whereby they were lost as much as, if not more than, any other Indian woman. As brought out lately by an Indian lady scholar, "Some social scientists have very rightly described the Moghul era as the dark age for women. By the end of this era women no longer enjoyed the freedom of the earlier times, and even within the family as a unit, their importance became nil. The pages of the history of this age are, figuratively

---

[10] *Das Frauenlebeir der Erde*, Wien, Pest, Leipzig, 1881; *Woman*, op.cit., vol.ii, p.260.

speaking, black in colour, due to the oppression meted out at this time".[11]

During this period, when the atmosphere was so vitiated that even the horrid acts of female infanticide had to be performed for self preservation, when even a marriage had to be performed secretly at the dead hours of night lest the new bride on way to her new home may be abducted enroute, when faith had lost all meaning and no two factions in this vast land could trust each other, another set of people form distant lands were sailing forth in quest of economic survival. That they found this soil bursting with dissension, *phoot,* ripe enough to burst out of its own, was enough motivation to find one's way like the fruit called *phoot,* through inevitable invitations, howsoever supercilious.

---

11 Malthi Sharma, *The Women's Decade* 1975-85, p.76, Joint Women's Programme, New Delhi, 1985.

10

THE EUROPEAN SEARCH FOR HEGEMONY AROUND THE WORLD

In the tumultuous period of the middle ages, the sword of Islam had also fanned out to the West. Having conquered the whole of North-West Africa, it embarked on Europe itself. Christianity faced extinction but after containment and ejection of Islam from Europe, the European princes, rode forth in the Crusades. The end of thcsc religious expeditions, however, brought to an end the short-lived Christian European unity. Soon different bands under their own banners set out in hunt for riches fighting as much with each other as with the natives they came in contact with.

"About the year 1150 a rumour spread through Europe that somewhere in Asia there existed a powerful Christian ruler by the name of Prester John (Presbyter Johannes), whose kingdom was called Kara Kitai. In a Europe which cut a rather poor figure beside the Moslem colossus, this mysterious 'priest-king' rapidly became a symbol of hope... he was sought for now in Asia, now in Africa, until the end of the fifteenth century". [1]

In the course of events, the Portuguese explorer Vasco da Gama showed the way to India in 1498. Later, the celebrated Albuquerque managed to capture Goa after a hard battle and made it the seat of the Portuguese power in Asia.

"Albuquerque's work must not be underestimated. His strategy can be summed up in three points: (1) the organisation of a real colony in Goa, where, in order to ensure Portuguese settlement, he did not hesitate to encourage marriage with native women; (2) the building of forts or strongholds at all the strategic points of the ocean; (3) the signing of treaties with the rulers of territories of importance for trade. This strategy, which aimed not at territorial

[1] Toussaint, op.cit., p.89

conquest but only at the control of trade routes, was to be adopted almost unchanged, at the beginning at least, by all the Western people who followed the Portuguese in the Indian Ocean".[2]

The Portuguese were closely followed by the Dutch, the English, the Danes, and the French. The beginning of the East India Company in India was modest. The watchwords were prudence and circumspection. Sir Thomas Roe, an envoy of the East India Company at the court of the Great Mogul, declared in 1616 that war and trade were incompatible. This, however, did not put a stop to infighting among the traders.

During the entire first half of the seventeenth century the situation of the English company in India remained somewhat precarious. Far from finding, as it had hoped, an outlet in the Indian markets for fabrics, and other English products, it was forced, on the contrary, to buy textiles from the Indians so as to exchange them for spices. A similar situation was faced by the other European India Companies. We thus see that for economic survival these companies were drawn inevitably into the path of imperialism. Holden Furber, an American, however, has drawn a contrary conclusion: "Economic contact between India and the West, was inevitable, but imperialism was not inevitable. It grew out of the weaknesses and diversities of Indian society, and in particular out of Indian powerlessness at sea." [3]

Thus in 1614, the Dutch, Jan Pieterzoon Coen could advise his directors: "Trade in India must be conducted and maintained under the protection and favour of your weapons, and weapons must be supplied from the profits enjoyed by the trade, so that trade cannot be maintained without war or war without trade." [4]

Not to be outdone, Gerald Aungier, chief of the English

---

[2] Toussaint, op.cit., p.105.

[3] H.Furber, *John Company at Work*, Cambridge, Mass., 1952, p. 321.

[4] F.B. Eldridge, *The Background of Eastern Sea Power, London*, 1948, p. 237.

at Bombay, wrote in 1669 to the directors of the company in London: "The time now requires you to manage your general commerce with the sword in your hands." [5] In 1687, the directors ordered their agents in India "to establish such a politie of civil and military power... as may be the foundation of a large, well grounded secure English dominion in India for all time to come." [6] Clearly, a very complete programme, and one that was to be carried out to the letter. And the intention was obviously not to colonise, like the Dutch, but to rule, like the Portuguese.

Throughout this period, and even earlier we find that the Christian missionaries did not lag behind in their effort to propagate their faith. On this, Toussaint says, "Back in the twelth century, as we know, those who had taken the route to the Orient in search of souls had very closely followed, and sometimes even preceded, those who had taken the same route in search of gold, and their accounts had contributed more than a little to Europe's information about the Eastern world. In the sixteenth century they had sailed out in caravels to spread the Gospel in the Portuguese possessions in Asia; and although they can be reporached with having lighted the fires of the Inquisition at Goa, they did on the other hand, present the Indian Ocean with an extraordinary and admirable missionary in the person of St. Francis Xavier, whose radiance itself was enough to excuse his confreres their momentary mistakes."[7] It is beyond the scope of this essay to bring out such ordeals by which, sad to say, the Protestants also brought ignominity to their religion. Suffice to say that, "There had been a serious attempt too, at home in Parliament to 'Christianise our Indian population' wholesale in order, it was said, 'to strengthen our hold on the country'. Such a proposal might well have started a mutiny in which the whole population of India would have taken

---

[5] Toussaint, op.cit., p.129.

[6] R.C. Majumdar, *An Advanced History of India*, London, 1956, p. 639.

[7] Toussaint, op.cit., p.185. On the Inquisition at Goa, see Dellon's account, *Voyage de M. Dellon avec sa relation de l'Inquisition de Goa*, 3 vols., Cologne, 1711.

part."[8] Toussaint adds, "Westerners, in using the decline of Asia to their own ends, employed not European but typically Asian methods. Moreover, as a consequence of that decline, the Orientals did not develop any inferiority complex, nor did the Westerners develop a complex of superiority. The East-West antithesis is a phonomenon of the nineteenth and not of the eighteenth century."[9]

In India, at the time of the collapse of the Mughal Empire only two imperial powers, England and France, remained in the hegemonic struggle. The French East India Company was not an independent body of merchants, but a department of government. Like many government departments in France at the time, it was badly administered. But the root cause of the failure of France, as of Portugal, was her loss of the command of the sea. This was fatal.

When ambitions clashed as in Africa the Europeans did not hesitate to hold the Berlin conference in 1884-85 to talk across the table under King Leopold II of Belgium and carved out their spheres of influence in the whole African continent so that their middle class lived better there than the lords back home. As for the poor and the 'wanted' persons, Columbus had already found a heaven in America in 1498. And for those who were the greatest criminals, languishing in prisons involving unnecessary drain on the state exchequer, Australia was much later in 1788 forced as the abode, though the expedition had reached there as early as in 1501. The rich American spends long time now in Europe to find where and how his poor ancestors lived. The Australian considers it an affront till today, if any one asks him of his ancestry.

While Western Europe's unity was forged with the demarcation of Africa, old feuds amongst them in India or elsewhere in Asia were also forgotten. On the British Empire in India a French economist, the Abbé de Pradt expressed his views

---

8 J.K. Stanford, *Ladies in the Sun*, The Galley Press, London, 1962, p. 109.

9 Toussaint, op.cit., p.152.

created a sensation. His argument can be summed up as follows :

> "Trade with India, burdensome for Europe, involved the use of metal currency and attracted the money Europe received from the New World. Now the only nation that had succeeded in dispensing with the sending of metals to India by the establishment there of sovereign rights was England... The more English sovereignty spread through India, the more she exempted Europe from the need to send capital into that country... it was in fact in the interest of all Europe to maintain British power in India." [10]

Toussaint concludes :

"The main fact to remember in the transition from the old colonialism to the new is the following. Whereas under the the fomer system it had been the East that in a certain sense 'exploited' the West by taking from it a vast quantity of metallic currency, henceforth it was the West that was to exploit the East, and in the full sense of the word... for the first time the European was able to impose his conditions and to invest his money profitably as he saw fit. It was thus that the East-West antithesis came about... [11]

Not much had been written on the East-West thesis or antithesis so long as the while rule prevailed. Now when writing the epilogue, the white man does not hesistate to make a complete study and their younger generation does not waver to give a frank view. What do we do? With the background of a 700 years' slavery in parts of our land, where can one find an indigenous analysis on the causes of our failure? It would be of interest to note here that though considered a late start, genuine efforts had been made in the West to make a comprehensive study on colonialism and and its effect. "Thanks to UNESCO, very real progress had been made in promoting closer cultural ties between East and West.

---

[10] M. de Pradt, *Les Trois Ages des colonies*, Paris, 1902, II, p. 452; Toussaint, op.cit., p. 193.
[11] Toussaint, op.cit., p.196.

There is no doubt that Europe has been taking more and more of an interest in the East and that orientalist bookshops in the large European cities find no lack of either books or customers. On the other hand, it would seem that in most of the countries of Asia and Africa there has been a dearth of serious works showing Europe in its true light."[12] We will here attempt a short look at the social aspects of this East-West antithesis.

---

12 Toussaint, op.cit., p.248.

11

FOR ST. GEORGE AND THE KING OF ENGLAND

The expansion of British power around the world excited strange views from those they came in contact with. There is an Arab saying that if one sees two fish fighting in the sea, one must look for the British for the trouble caused. The Iraqis remind you of instances where numerous riots were got triggered off by the British betwen the Sunnis and the Shias even on such flimsy grounds that the bone of a Shia was implanted in the grave of a Sunni causing affront to a whole segment of society. The characteristic attitude of the peoples of western Asia towards the English is well illustrated by the words of an old Arab sheikh, who frankly said to one of the members of Colonel Chesney's Euphrates Expedition, in 1837, "the English are like ants: if one finds a bit of meat, a hundred follow." [1]

Napoleon summed up the British as a nation of shopkeepers. Let us see the depth to which they could go down. Maurice Collis says, "The drug traffic had been fostered by the East India Company with careful deliberation...[2] and a monopoly created by forcing growers to sell the whole crop to the Company... A decision was taken at the time of Warren Hastings (1772-1785) to decrease home consumption and develop an export trade. It was well known that the Chinese would buy; the Portuguese had been selling them for generations opium they procured at Malwa... Though opium was also exported from Turkey to China, chiefly by

---

1 W.F. Ainsworth, *Narrative of the Euphrates Expedition*, II, 197; *British Routes to India*, H.L. Hoskins, 1966, p. 193.

2 The opium poppy is probably a native of Southern Europe and Western Asia. On the use of opium in India, Tod brought out in 1820, "Whatever may be the antiquity of this drug for medicinal uses it may be asserted that its abuse (in India) is comparitively recent, or not more than three centuries back. In none of the ancient heroic poems of Hindustan is it ever alluded to". Tod, op.cit., vol.ii, p. 507.

the Americans, this brand was very inferior and had only a small market, so that the Company had obtained in fact a world monopoly..." [3]

The Company's revenue from their sales of it at the Calcutta auctions rose steadily. In 1973, it stood at a quarter of a million pounds and in 1832 at just under one million, a figure which representing as it did about a sixth of the whole Indian revenue, was clearly of great importance to the administration.

It is not that we could escape this inferno. Tod made an outcry when he spoke (c.1820), "The feverish excitement produced by our monopoly of the drug has extended its culture in every direction... The predatory system, which succeeded Moghul despotism, soon devastated this fair region and gradually restricted agricultural pursuits... till at length even these were confined to a bare sustenance of the families of the cultivator who then found a substitute in the poppy...if we fail to restore the moral energies of her population (Rajpootana)... of this fine region and noble race we might say as Byron does of Greece —

" 'Tis Greece – but living Greece no more ! "

"It is to be hoped that the legislature at home will perceive that a perseverence in this pernicious traffic is consistent neither with our honour, our interest nor with humanity". [4]

In 1839 began the first 'opium war' resulting in 1842 in the treaty of Nanking, by the terms of which the opium trade received official sanction. Commenting on this victory of free trade, Palmerston, the British Prime Minister, wrote the same year: "There is no doubt that this event, which will form an epoch in the progress of the civilisation (sic) of the human races, must be attended with the most important advantages to the commercial

---

3 *Foreign Mud*, Faber and Faber Ltd., London, pp. 74-76.

4 Tod, op.cit., Vol. ii, pp. 506-511.

interest of England." [5]

Be it said to the credit of the British that though they masterminded and adopted the most abominable, despicable and heinous means to amass wealth causing emasculation of the whole Chinese race, they did not themselves fall a victim to their evil pursuit. Perhaps love for wine, women and sports, apart from quest for money and power, kept them out of the tentacles of opium. And we, who have now become accomplices in the chain of the golden crescent of Iran, Afghanistan and Pakistan in their 'drug trafficking', have not been able to prevent our educated youth, not to talk of the lowest, from becoming victims of this vice in our search for easy money. One could have understood if the Chinese had taken to drugs-peddling to settle old scores, but why we Indians, who under the Sahibs' power were made to grow more opium, the curse on humanity, and are aware of its consequences, allow ourselves to be the carriers of the disease, a slow and vitriolic scourage on the whole universe including ourselves?

The British came to India when no central authority was left therein. Petty regional lords were at logger heads with each other. It prompted Tod to admit, "Our position in the East has been, and continues to be, in which conquest forces herself upon us." [6] Nevertheless, for the British the transition from being a merchant to a ruler was no mean achievement. Economic adventure, statecraft, military professionalism and use of compliant clerics apart, there was no dearth of dedication or heroism for 'St. George and the King of England'. It culminated in a Bill being brought forward in the British Parliament in February, 1876, to add to the titles of the Queen that of "Empress of India." In answer to the strong opposition which developed to the measure on its first reading, Disraeli said (March 9, 1876):

---

[5] M. Greenberg, *British Trade and the Opening of China*, 1800-1842, Cambridge, 1951, p. 215.

[6] Tod. op. cit; vol. i, p. 101

"... It is desired in India ...It is anxiously expected... let the people of India feel that there is a sympathetic (sic) chord between us and them, and do not let Europe suppose for a moment that there are any in this House who are not deeply conscious of the importance of the Indian Empire... By passing this Bill ... the House will show, in a manner which is unmistakable, that they look upon India as one of the most precious possessions of the crown, and their pride that it is a part of her Empire and governed by her imperial throne. The frontiers of Russia are only a few days' march from those of Her Majesty in India... This announcement... will justify in a manner which cannot be mistake, that the Parliament of England is resolved to uphold the Empire in India"[7]

It is only fair that we proceed to have a glimpse at the life of those who managed to achieve the near impossible task of ruling over another nation, 7000 miles away from their land, the latter always remaining their home.

---

[7] *Hansards's Parl. Deb*:, CCXXVII, p.1727; TE Kebbel, *Selected Speeches of the Rt. Hon. the Earl of Beaconsfield*, 2 vols., London, 1882, II, p.239.

12

THE SAHIBS, THE MEMSAHIBS AND THE SLAVES

We shall now have a look at as to how the white man found the prevalent conditions in India when he arrived here, how he adjusted to and transformed these to suit his convenience and how the Memsahib fitted in the whole panorama. The early merchants never dreamt what their trade could achieve. It would be better that we go through some of their own letters written back home as well as observations recorded by themselves in their own language to get an insight into the travails gone through. [1]

THE BEGINNING

"Mr. Edwardes presented the Kinge (the Mogul Emperor Jehangir) a mastife, and speakinge of the dog's courage, the Kinge cawsed a younge leopard to be brought to make tryall, which the dogge soe pinchtt, thatt fewer howres after the leoparde dyed. Synce, the Kinge of Persia, with a present, sent heather haulfe a dozen dogges— the Kinge cawsed boares to be brought to fight with them, puttings two or three dogges to a boare, yet none of them seased; and rememberinge his owne dogge, sentt for him, who presently fastened on the boare, so disgraced the Persian doggs, wherewith the Kinge was exceedingly pleased."

Letter from Kerridge,
President at Surat, 1612

Such were the English at their first appearance on the Western coast of India. It must be confessed that the natives had before them a strange variety of models from which to form in their minds the character of an Englishman. Roe and Herbert, the acute

---

[1] Cf. *The Sahibs*, Edited by Hilton Brown, William Hodge and Co. Ltd., London, 1948; *British Social Life in India*, Dennid Kincaid.

diplomatist and the polished gentleman; Best, Downton, and other valiant mariners; the inquiring and literary Kerridge; hard-headed, ungrammatical and religious Joseph Salbank; wine-bibbing Rastell; Mildenhall, cheat and assassin; preachers of gospellers half Anglican and half Zuinglian; orthodox chaplains; a few scamish reckless travellers; and piratical merciless captains — such a medley could scarely leave any well-defined impressions upon the native mind. Probably opinions were decided by circumstances. The jovial Jehangeer found that an Englishman was well-trained courtier and good boon-companion; the *bunyas* of Surat found that he was a clever tradesman, and a hard driver of a bargain. But doubtless at first the population feeling was one of fear, afterwards of contempt. Hindoos and Mussulmans considered the English a set of cow-eaters and fire-drinkers, vile brutes, fiercer than the mastiffs which they brought with them, who would fight like Eblis, cheat their own fathers, and exhange with the same readiness a broadside of shot and thrusts of boarding-pikes, or a bale of goods and a bag of rupees.

ANDERSON

The Factory had about a score of good Dogs for Game, of the Engligh Brood, and the Company allowed each of them about 2 1b of boyl'd Rice daily, but now they are better Husbands of their Money, and have discharged all their Dogs and other Superfluities except one good old Custom of treating Strangers that come there from Europe, with pretty black female Dancers, who are very active in their Dancing, and free in their Conversation, where Shame is quite out of Fashion.

HAMILTON (circa 1720)

PERSONAL LIFE

I am now to fulfil my promise, to give you a particular account of the day, as it is commonly spent by an Englishman in Bengal. About the hour of seven in the morning, his doorkeeper opens the gate, and the viranda is free to his *circars*, peons, *chubdar*... writers and solicitors. The head-bearer and *jemmadar* enter the hall and his bedroom at eight o'clock. A lady quits his side, and is conducted by a private straircase, either to her own apartment or out of the yard. The moment the master throws his legs out of bed, the whole posse in waiting rush into his room... In about half an hour after undoing and taking off his long drawers, a clean shirt, breeches, stockings, and slippers are put upon his body... without any greater exertion on his own part, than if he was a statue. The barber enters, shaves him, cuts his nails, and cleans his ears... The superior then walks in state to his breakfasting parlour in his waistcoat; is seated; the *consumah* makes and pours out his tea, and presents him with a plate of bread or toast. The hair-dresser comes behind and begins his operation, while the *houccabadar* softly slips the upper end of the snake of tube of the *houcca* into his hand. While the hair-dresser is doing his duty, the gentleman is eating, sipping and smoking by turns. By and by his *banian* presents himself with humble salaams... These ceremonies are continued till perhaps ten o'clock; when, attended by his cavalcade, he is conducted to his palanquin, and preceded by eight to ten *Chubdars*, *harcarrahs* and peons... they move off at a quick amble... He... pursues his other engagements till two o'clock, when he and his company sit down... to a good dinner, each attended by his own servant. And the moment the glasses are introduced, regardless of the company of ladies, the *houccabadars* enter, each with a *houcca*, and presents the tube to his master, watching behind and blowing the fire the whole time. As it is expected that they shall return to supper, at four o'clock they begin to withdraw... and step into their palanquins; so that... the master is left to go to his bed-room when he is instantly undressed to his shirt and his long drawers put on; and he lies down on his bed where he sleeps till about seven or eight o'clock; then the former ceremony is repeated... his *houccabadar* presents the tube to his hand, he is placed at the tea-table and the hair-dresser performs his duty as before. After tea, he puts on a handsome coat, and pays visits of ceremony to the ladies; returns a little before ten o'clock; supper being served at ten. The company keep together till between twelve and one in the morning, preserving great sobriety and decency; and when they depart, our hero is conducted to his bedroom. With no greater exertions than these, do the Company's servants amass the most splendid fortunes.

MACKINTOSH,
Travels in Europe, Asia and Africa (1779.)

THE RIPOSTE

The fifty-fifth letter of this author (Mackintosh above) is a strong but highly caricature likeness of the manners of the Europeans in general who serve in Asia. The pomp and state he reports them to live in comes but to the share of those few, who live long enough to rise, by slow degrees... to the highest offices in the State. The lazy and indelicate custom of being dressed and undressed in the manner he describes, never is practised by any but such as grow very corpulent, and not always by them: it was a sight so rare, that I always used to ridicule and laugh at the very few lazy good-natured fellows whom I saw indulge themselves in it. The very pointed description which he gives and applies generally, made me endeavour to recollect from whom he drew it, and I now remember that he was lodged and boarded gratis, in the most open generous and friendly manner, by a plump good-natured hospitable soul as ever existed, who loves a convivial life...In general, the young gentlemen, as soon after their arrival as they can, muster money to buy a horse, ride from a little before daylight until eight o'clock then breakfast and go directly to the public offices, where they write hard till two or three o'clock at noon, then dine, and if all their daily business is done, they drink tea, visit the ladies, and perhaps dance with them or sup with them, or, which is more common, attend them in their visitings, which is always in the evening; after which they go home, and are fast asleep by twelve o'clock.

PRICE,
Observations and Remarks (On Mackintosh's Travels 1782)

TIME AND SPACE

1825—The Madras mail to Calcutta, by land, was done in 10 days 17-3/4 hours,

1826.— From Bombay to Calcutta, an express mail was done in 11-1/2 days.

The news of the death of the Princess Charlotte, which took place on November 6th, 1817, was only known in Bombay on February 28th, 1818, and the death of George III, which took place on January 29th, 1820, was not announced there until May

JAMES DOUGLAS

THE LAND AND THE PEOPLE

...I asked one lady what she had seen of the country and the natives since she had been in India. "Oh, nothing!" said she: "thank goodness, I know nothing at all about them, nor I don't wish to: really I think the less one sees and knows of them the better!"

Letters frrom Madras (1837)

15th August 1837 — Why should I keep a journal? There is nothing to relate in the monotony of an Indian life at home. The weary, heavy day, the hot and sleepless night, the excessive heat of the weather, the relaxation of the body, the heaviness of mind, the want of interest in everything, the necessity of a colder air and a colder climate to restring nerves that are suffering from fifteen years' residence in India; all this I feel most strongly, and must either return to England or go to the hils to recruit my weary frame.

MRS PARKES

(A friend noted : "But she has just given us a learned and exhaustive discourse on Krishna, and proceeds at once to an equally full account of buffalow and tiger hunting in Assam, neither of which shows any want of interest".)

The same lady wrote later:

12th December, 1844—How I love this roaming life on the river, with the power of stopping at any picturesque spot!... I have a great sympathy for Dr. Syntax, and perfectly comprehend the delight he took even in a picturesque horse-pond. India would have driven him wild; — it is the country of the picturesque. How I love this life in the wilderness! I shall never be content to vegetate in England.

MRS PARKES

THE WIVES

16th February, 1838. I perceive the officers' (army) ladies are curioulsy different from the civilians. The civil ladies are generally very quiet, rather languid, speaking in almost a whisper, simply dressed, almost always ladylike and comme-il-faut, not pretty, but pleasant and nice-looking, rather dull, and give one very hard work in pumping for conversation... The military ladies, on the contrary, are always quite young, pretty, noisy, affected... while they are alone with me after dinner, they talk about suckling their babies, the disadvantages of scandal, "the Officers, " and " the Regiment" and when the gentlemen come into the drawing-room, they invariably flirt with them most furiously...

Letters from Madras

1st November, 1839. The Europeans here (Bangalore) are chiefly military, and the ladies are different from any I have seen yet. The climate does not tempt them to the dawdling class of idleness, so they ride about in habits made according to the uniform of their husbands' regiments, and do various spirited things of that kind. There are some of a very superior class — almost always the ladies of the colonels or principal officers in the European regiments. These seem never to become Indianized, and have the power of being exceedingly useful. Some of them keep up schools for the English soldiers' children, girls especially — superintend them, watch over the soldiers' wives, try to keep and encourage them in good ways, and are quite a blessing to their poor country-women.

Letters from Madras

THE AFTERMATH OF THE MUTINY

The good old *hookah* days are past ; cheroots and pipes have now usurped the place of the aristocratic silver bowl, the cut-class goblets, and the twisted glistening snake with silver or amber mounthpiece... The race of Eurasians is not so freely supplied with recruits... There is now no *bee-bee's* house — a sort of European *zenana*... There are now European rivals to those ladies (the native kept women) at some stations. It was the topic of conversation the other day at mess that the colonel of a regiment had thought it right to prohibit one of his officers from appearing publicly with an unauthorised companion at the band parade; and the general opinion was that he had no right to interfere. But the society of the station does interfere in such cases, and though it does not mind *beebees* or their friends, it rightly taboos him who entertains their white rivals.

RUSSEL (1858)

But the problem of nurse or *ayah* pales, all too soon, before one of infinitely greater moment — the rival claims of India and England; of husband and child. Sooner or later the lurking shadow of separation takes definite shape; asserts itself as a harsh reality; a grim presence, whispering the inevitable question; "Which shall it be?" A question not lightly to be answered; if indeed, in generalised form, it can be answered at all. Every woman, when her time comes, must face it frankly, from her own individual standpoint; and thresh out her own individual answer according to her lights. An unsatisfactory one it is bound to be, at best; and countless brave hearts have been strained to breaking point during those bitter hours of indecision.

MAUD DIVER (1909)

A dear little lady I met the other day, talking about her sister Memsahibs, said airily, "Of course we very soon lose complexions, manners and morals". She could afford to say so, it being so obviously untrue in her case. I think it is just this, that the women who are pure gold grow more charming, but the pinchbeck wears off very soon.

OLIVE DOUGLAS (1913)

THE PARTING

And so I am going home, home to my own bleak, kindly land, "place of all weathers that end in rain" I am going home to my own people ...; and I am going to you. And the queer thing is, I can't feel glad. I am so home-sick for India.[2]

OLIVE DOUGLAS (1913)

* * *

We have gone through a wide ranging spectacle, wherein man's nature is shown to take different forms, from the offshoots of cacti to the choicest roses. Now let us have a look at another pageant, more complex and captivating in which we see an endles variety of beautiful colours and forms which ladies embrace as naturally as the lilies. To see their vibrant, delightful or pathetic state, in different hues, some wine-coloured or golden-rayed, others scarlet, orange-crimson or even black, with few spotless white symbols of purity, like the Easter or madonna lilies, we will go through some excerpts from *Ladies in the Sun* ,[3] on the life of the Memsahibs in India whose thoughts Rudyard Kipling so aptly describes:-

"With every shift of every wind
The homesick memories come
From every quarter of mankind
Where I have made me a home."

Stanford, J. K., starts by wondering, what was it like, particulrly for a woman, to embark in a sailing ship bound for India round the Cape, and what sort of a life could she expect in India if she got there. By 1750 the picture of these women's lives becomes a little clearer. No young writer came out to India married. He started his carreer on a pittance. He was expected to behave himself and keep away from 'the Black Town'. Wives were strongly discouraged. To marry these men, women of good education and standing must have had little or no encouragement, with always the

---

2 The same nostalgia of sweet and sour memories lingered on in many white men and women who were forced to leave India in 1947. Some got reconciled with reality but few could mentally go back to the drudgery of plebian life.

3 J.K. Stanford, op.cit.

chance that on the voyage out they would be picked up by pirates. Convent-reared Protuguese girls destined for Goa had found themselves in a slave market earlier.

"English women in India were few and only the venturesome or the very devoted were undeterred by the dangers of the voyage. For a hundred and fifty years the men had either married into the Protuguese families already domiciled in Madras and Surat or taken native mistresses. Blotted pedigress were as common as one might expect right up to the end of the eighteenth century. As time went on, the Company's servants on the Bombay side attempted to import 'gentle women and other women' for the marriage market, as the Protuguese at Goa had done before them. These women were not given dowry as had been the Portuguese custom but on arrival were guaranteed their 'diet', board and lodging for one year. If they failed to marry someone within that time, the Company either frowned severely on their morals or threatened to send them home, as much later match-making mammas did to their awkward daughters who had sailed out to India with the 'fishing-fleet'.[4]

To continue our walk on Stanford's esplanade encircling the lilies of all tints :-

"Men in desolate up-country stations seem often to have married precipitately out of a sense of loneliness. Of one couple met at Simla just after their marriage, Emily Eden notes that the husband was 'an object of much commiseration. Not but what he is very happy probably, but he married the very first young lady that came up to the hills this season; she was uncommon ordinary then and nothing can look worse, somehow, than she does now. ... When they have been two or three years in a solitary station, they should not propose to the very first girl they see.' In short, women were arriving in increasing numbers, spinsters were scarce, and the old open concubinage with natives which had prevailed in the eighteenth century was becoming outmoded. Mixed marriages too with the Portuguese families in Madras or with women of equally uncertain origin were also frowned on. It had long been necessary

---

4 J.K. Stanford, op.cit., p.3.

for a writer or an ensign to obtain the Governor's leave to marry...

"But the 'pure' Europeans were rather like the Boers. They did not admit Indians to their clubs or houses. They had separate wards in hospitals, separate hotels, separate dak-bungalows and reserved compartments on trains and in railway restaurants. Only very rarely did they entertain Indians at their table. And we may be sure that this strict apartheid was not only endorsed but instigated by their women folk. Just as the first warning any young writer received in the eighteenth century was 'to keep away from the Black Town', so now the young civil servant at the start of his career was straitly warned not only about the colour-bar but the possible lures of some faintly tinged but designing Eurasian damsel. She might be the daughter, under the rose, of one of his commissioners or of a general, but she was taboo...[5]

Apartheid, yes, to the extent of enforcing the rule 'Dogs and Indians not allowed' in some exclusive places, but no amount of taboo could banish or interdict intromissions which took varied forms. 'My Fair Lady', in some cases, contributed to the build-up of the Empire by making herself available in plenty to those who were serving the crown in the parched land far away from 'home'. Her patriotism was more evident in hill stations where she used to be sent to rest and recoup, away from the horrid heat of the plains, when the poor husband remained stuck at his post down below. However, she was far too outnumbered to keep all the chicks under her. Most of the Officers' Messes had the custom that if a solitary gentleman, devoid of any company, was forced to eat alone, champagne was served to him 'on the house'. But the sparkle of the grapes was hardly any substitute and could not soothen some hardened spines. John Masters[6] speaks of one such stallion in a hurry who would announce his entry in the Mess by shouting *Qoi hai*, whereupon the *abdar* would instantly appear, to be ordered to 'Bring large brandy and wash the sweeper's daughter'. There is something in the flora that interwines an Eve which gives stimulus

[5] J.K. Stanford, op.cit., pp. 129 - 131.
[6] Bugles and a Tiger.

to a man forcing him to break all barriers to reach her.

Lower down, any wine seller in an old Cantonment describes how after consuming a tot of rum the Tommies found the street itself good enough as a beach to relax with poor native girls of the have-nots. The civilian official, when in need, could go to the nearest Railway Club, which in those days catered for the off-springs of heros of yore. These Anglo Indians (not to be confused with the early Britishers in India) were engaged in manning this essential service of the Crown with their females lessening the burden of heat on the little sahibs, yet their great devotion rarely produced any union of lasting nature. The British military officer was more authoritative. John Masters [7] says that when in need they had just to give a tinkle to the Matron of the local Military Hospital to provide the required number of nurses as companions for the day and the Matron considered it her bounden duty to fulfil her obligation. The ban generated by the Mutiny eventually vapoured out over passage of time with the establishment of WAACI, female auxiliary corps of the Army, mostly Anglo-Indian. However, as the British left soon after, unnecessary stigma remained attached to these children of discarded sacrifice and disowned petulance. In time to come the British 'generosity' could find a refuge for hundreds of them in Australia though the doors of England were never opened for them even when hordes of blackies of India, Pakistan, Sri Lanka and West Indies were flooding inside. What a mockery of racial ostracism! As if these products of their own passions could pollute the purity of their race !

---

[7] Op. cit.

As we have seen by the time the British established their trading posts firmly in India, the Moghul Empire had already been fragmented. The British traders seized the opportunities available in our land and soon started behaving like any foreign invader, concentrating their energies towards the establishment and expansion of the their empire conjointly with furtherance of economic interests. The already mutilated Indians were bled white. In these conditions it was not difficult to find native women of lower classes to meet the personal needs of the rulers. Gradually British women were inducted in India in small batches to keep the interests of at least the ruling elite on a more even keel. These British women led a very uncertain and difficult life. They, however, on their part did not spare any effort to wean away their gentry from local women. The major event that prompted complete segregation in any social intercourse with the Indians was the mutiny in 1857. From then onwards only as much contact was kept with the natives as was essential for administrative control or economic subjugation. Everything else was relegated to the backgound. The social plight of the natives became a popular subject of contemptuous conversation during the evening cocktails. On the pretext of non-interference in religion, local customs, howsoever abhorent and against established tenets, were upheld. It was not a case of maintaining old customs and traditions. It was a process of burying down fine traditions of the *Vedic* period, the golden age for women, under the debauched tombstone of degenerated customs. Yet, one must admit that when things became so perverse for women that it called for action on humanitarian grounds, the British listened to the wise counsel of social reformers like Raja Ram Mohan Roy and Swami Dayanand and enacted several laws to improve the position of women. Some of these enactments were the Act prohibiting *Sati* in 1850, Caste Disabilities Removal Act, 1850, and Hindu Widow Remarriage Act, 1856. The Special Marriage Act III of 1872 enabled one to marry outside one's own caste; the Married Women's Property Act, 1874 provided for maintenance and limited status; The Child Marriage Act 1929 raised the marriageable ages both for males and females; the Hindu Gains of Earning Act, 1930 provided that the earnings of the woman were her property; Hindu Women's Right to Property to Property Act, 1937 made the proviso that the widows shall have the same rights as the husband had during the lifetime. The Christian Marriage Act, 1872, the Parsee Marriage and Divorce Act, 1936, and the Dissolution of Muslim Marriage Act, 1939 made laws in respect of these communities. Unfortunately, these limited piecemeal legal reforms did not bring about much improvement in the actual status of woman in India. No energy was wasted by the rulers to enforce these laws which, however, did serve the prupose of exhibiting their noble intent that they were there in India to discharge their obligations towards the white man's burden! If the natives preferred to live in darkness, it was their lookout and it was not for the rulers to waste their time and effort towards enforcing a better social order.

It was at this time that Gandhiji appeared on the scene. When one looks back, it appears that his emergence was the greatest gift the British unknowingly generated for India and Humanity. Gandhiji not only fought against imperialism and economic slavery but proved to be the only Indian after a lapse of ages who brought woman back in the mainstream. The Mahatma encouraged women to leave the shackles of home and involved them in the freedom struggle in the frontline alongwith their men. The result was that, unlike in the West, the Indian women did not have to demand and fight for their rights but got them through the Constituion of free India. The Hindu Code Bill is one of the most progressive legislations passed in favour of women without their having to assert their rights for it. The Mahatma was snatched away too soon after independence. Not much thereafter, dark medieval clouds began to lour over the aspirations of the Indian woman. Could she draw any inspiration from those of her gender who had been in a position to improve women's destiny ? A glimpse would reveal that any great expectations from women in power have by and large remained delusive everywhere.

13

SHE

In our walk through the passage of time, we have seen the best and the worst rulers who have governed anytime, anywhere in the whole world. Somehow, for different reasons, woman did not get a fair deal from either of them. One would have thought that when 'She' got a chance to be an absolute ruler, a way would be paved for the uplift of her whole kind. Has it been so?

There is Lord Acton's durable dictum that 'Power corrupts and absolute power corrupts absolutely'. Most of the kings and conquerors, princes and men in power all over the world, have considered the custom to acquire more females as synonymous with and symbolic of their authority. But then sometimes some got so engrossed in the pursuit of increasing the number of symbols that they became totally ignorant of the basic craft of rulership.

It is said, that Louis XIII, son of the wise and formidable Henry IV who reigned over France from 1610 to 1643, fulfilled his passion for fame by exploring more of the tender regions of all kinds than acquiring terrestrial territory. Yet he remained oblivious of the lunar rainbow as his famous last words indicate, " Woman! I do not know you as yet".

What about the independent well-known queens? Did they exercise any restraint on themselves or on their absolute power by not overwhelming the opposite sex? The affairs of Cleopatra (69-30 BC) are looked upon as expected from a queen of that era and we ignore whether it was she, Ceasar or Antony who came out better. There have been other queens also, who have wielded supreme authority.

Few rulers of the fair sex whose ventures, if they were ordinary mortals, might have earned for them the euphemism as by Elizabeth I of England (1533-1603) of being 'The Great Queen of a Great Age'. Of remarkable physical vigour, masculine in her coarseness of word and action, her craze for the spicy side of life was not restricted to her Surrey palace *Nonsuch*, but all her sins were forgotten when she founded the East India Company [1] that laid the foundations of the Empire, having already settled scores with the Papal Queen Mary of Scots. Never married, her suitors, alternatively loved and scolded, were numerous even until she was old. On call by the affairs of the State, she forced herself to sign the death warrant of one of her favourite suitors, the ill-fated Earl of Essex. Killings are part of the game of love and war. If the darned weather of Britain could not dampen her spleen, the bitter cold of Russia couldnot withhold a more voracious *Tsarina* of the same name Elizabeth (1709-1762) who proved more ruthless in her demands. Young cadets from the Russian military officers' academy were selected to prove their loyalty within the precincts of the Royal parlour and those whe failed to pay fitting respects to the royal standards were marched off to hibernate, if they could, in Siberia unless relieved of the torture by immediate fatal disposal.

Later, had Victoria of England not been so much directly involved in becoming an Emperatrix, perhaps her demeanour may have been different or more would have been told about her.

In India, women had little chance to assert themselves in imperial regalia except when forced to during regency. The not-so-well-known small time queen Qudsia Begum invited the wrath of of her whole ethnic group when she preferred an Abyssinian to any of her own in her court. The famous Rani of Jhansi is only remerbered for her role as a fighter for independence. As for the other absolute female power of our time, Mrs. Indira Gandhi, [2] we

---

[1] On 31 Dec. 1600, a Royal Charter incorporated the Company under the title of "*The Governor and Company of Merchants of London trading into the East Indies.*"

[2] Her presence has been a source of great inspiration to many women around the world. When a group of disheartened feminists lamented the failure to get their legitimate demands accepted and expressed the fear that some of them would be arrested, Mrs. Jehan Sadat, wife of the then President of Egypt, who was behind them, instantly replied, "If you go to prison, I will go with you. Indira Gandhi once said, 'It is true women sometimes go too far, but it's only when you go too far that others

are deprived of any intimate knowlege of personal affairs because Mr. M.O. Mathai, who was PPS to Nehru, conveniently did not get published the chapter on "She" in his book though he publicised everything else that a master valet does come to know of. Perhaps these papers would see the light of the day as Maulana Azad's sought after 30 pages have. These latter papers have hardly elaborated on Lady Edwina Mountbatten's influence on his 'friend and comrade' Nehru. For the time being let us see part of the speech delivered by Nehru at a State banquet given in honour of Lord and Lady Mountbatten on 20 June, 1948, on the eve of their departure from India to visualise the depth of emotions. "To you Madam, I should like to address myself also. The gods or some good fairy gave you beauty and high intelligence, and grace and charm and vitality, great gifts, and she who possesses them is a great lady wherever she goes. But unto those that have, even more shall be given, and they gave you something which was even rarer than those gifts, the human touch, the love of humanity, the urge to serve those who suffer and who are in distress, and this amazing mixture of qualities resulted in a radiant personality and in the healer's touch..."[3] Perhaps, no better tribute has ever been paid publicly to any lady.

Later, Mr. John Kenneth Galbraith, the Ambassador of the USA, was not restrainted by any personal friendship when he wrote his *Ambassador's Journal.* On the forthcoming visit of Mrs. Jacqueline Bouvier Kennedy (J.B.K.) in March '62 he said, "The President had told me that the case and management of Mrs. Kennedy involved a good deal of attention, and he is quite right... I was also more than a little troubled by the very practical fact that anything that went wrong on this trip would go very promptly to the White House..." The Ambassador personally inspected the guest house converted for J.B.K. which he found "very chic... refurnished with wonderful charm." The lady, however, moved

---

listen' ". These words were enough to sustain the struggle. Jehan Sadat, A Woman of Egypt, Simon and Schuster, New York, 1987, p.357.

[3] *Independence and After*, Govt of India, Aug, 1949, p. 370. In this collection of speeches by Nehru of over 400 pages, there is not one related to the women of India.

into a suite at the Prime Minister's residence.

One month after the visit, the ambassador recorded, "Last Thursday night, today being Saturday, Kitty (his wife) and I took Angie (Angie Dickinson, the star in the film *Jessica*) over to have Rhine wine with the German Ambassador and then went on in the early evening to see Nehru. He seemed to be making a good recovery from his illness and was much pleased by the visit. There are few men, myself possibly excluded, who more enjoy the company of good-looking women, and as he relaxed and expanded, the five minute call ran on thrity or forty minutes. I noticed, incidentally, that in his upstairs sitting room where he has the pictures of the really important people in his life—Gandhi, Motilal Nehru (his father), Tagore and Edwina Mountbatten — there is now a significant addition to wit: Mrs. Jacqueline B. Kennedy. It is the picture of J.B.K. and the Prime Minister walking arm in arm in the White House garden."[4] Both Edwina and Jacqueline were domineering ladies in their times but hardly any better Indo-Western amity appeared on the scene !

Leaving this diversion aside, one cannot fail to observe that no betterment in the life of the fair ones has accrued during the time when feminism had better chance to assert itself. One may ignore the lack of empathy or sympathy for women from a Benazir Bhutto who sat on an uncertain chair under the fear that the *mullahs* would pull the carpet away from underneath anytime if she chose to be less dogmatic. What about the Iron Lady, Margaret Thatcher? Was there any improvement done for the British women during her long tenure? Be that as it may, by and large, woman everywhere remained at ease so long as she received the attention she was entitled to. It is the hungary wolf, whoe uncontrolled virility led him astray making him neglect her, who sowed the seeds of discord and discontentment. Women in advancing countries fought for their dues though more often than not their efforts remained marginalised. Their varying success, however, did not result in any corresponding diminution in the ultra-sensual activities of their

---

[4] *Galbraith*, op.cit., pp. 332, 353.

counterpart. It is a paradox that women who rose against the sexual vagaries of their opposite number have themselves become active accomplices in the proliferation of some abnormalities. We need to have a look at the aberrations which cause disgust and still overwhelm part of humankind.

Let us start from the lowest.

14

THE FIRST WOMAN PANDORA AND UNISEXUAL UNISON

The ancient Greek mythology, so well narrated by Homer and Virgil, is full of pulsating episodes, with instincts shown to wander beyond perception which perhaps is a common denominator in all mystic narrations. A concise and simple acount of the origin of Heaven, Earth and Man is attempted here with analogous names in Roman mythology, where feasible, given in brackets.

In the beginning of things, so the ancient Greeks believed, all was chaos. Gradually objects began to take form. First appeared Uranus, the Sky and Gaea, the Earth. Uranus, the first ruler of the world, took Gaea to wife. Among their many children were 12 huge Titans; three brothers called Cyclopes who had only one eye apiece; and Briareus and his two brothers, who were strong, and had 100 hands and 50 heads each. Uranus detested his children, and thrust them into Tartarus, the vast abysss below the earth. But Gaea called on the Titans, to rise against their father, and Krones (Saturn) the craftiest, made himself the ruler. Rhea, his sister, became his wife.

Zeus (Jupiter) was the son of Kronos and Rhea. He had two brothers, Poseidon (Neptune) and Hades (Pluto). Hestia (Vesta), Demeter (Ceres) and Hera (Juno) were his sisters. He dethroned his father, the king of the gods, and drove the Titans out of heaven. After the expulsion of Titans, Zeus was allotted the empire of heaven and air, Poseidon that of the sea and Hades wa given that of the infernal regions. The earth was left under the joint power of the three, but Zeus was supreme over all. At his palace on Mount Olympus in Greece, the gods met to settle the affairs of men. Zeus, after marrying his sister, Hera (Juno), married other goddesses. Among Zeus's many children were Apollo, god of light, youth and manly beauty and his twin sister Artemis (Diana), the huntress, goddess of chase who was never conquered by love. Apollo's mother was goddess Leto (Latona). Dionysus (Bacchus) was from another mother, Semale. Heracles (Hercules) was born from the mortal Alcmene, grand-daughter of Perseus. The goddess Hera was hostile to Hercules from his birth, and sent two serpants to destroy him in his cradle, but the infant strangled them with his hands.

For Zeus sky was the limit for love but Hera was not made of lesser mettle. She was not deceived when Zeus, to protect his beloved maiden Io from her jealousy, changed her into a heifer and made her swim across the strait of "Bosporus", in Greek meaning "Ox - Ford", but Hera tormented goddess Io until she was restrored to her human form to settle the matter. The beautiful nymph, Callisto, also aroused the suspicion of Hera. To protect Callisto, Zeus changed her into bear. But Arcas, Callisto's son, while hunting in the forest, was about to kill his mother, whom he took for an ordinary bear, when Zeus in pity changed him into a little bear and placed them both in heavens. There they are to this day, the Little Bear (Ursa Minor), the tip of whose tail is the North (or Pole) Star, and the Great Bear (Ursa Major), whose tail and saddle form the group known as the Plough, because the stars form that shape.

Hera was no less relenting when more challenges were thrown in her way. The story goes that at a feast where the gods and goddesses were celebrating the marriage of Peleus (grandson of Zeus and later father of Achilles) and Thetis (the sea nymph), an univited goddess, Eris, goddess of discord, threw among the guests an apple of gold which was inscribed, 'A gift for the fairest of all'. Naturally enough, the goddesses could not agree among themselve who merited the apple. The cause of envy and contention was claimed by the three goddesses of beauty, Aphrodite (Venus), goddess of love, who sprang full-grown from the sea-foam, Athena (Minerva), who sprang fully armed from the head of Zeus; goddess of storms, of war and wisdom, of spinning and weaving, and of agriculture, and protectress of cities, and Hera, the Queen goddess and guardian of women.

When the strife became bitter, Paris, the son of King Priam of Troy, was called upon to award the prize of beauty. Hera promised him power and riches if he would decide in her favour and Athena offered him glory and renown in war. But when Aphrodite whispered to him that if awarded the prize, she would give him the love of the most beautiful women in the world, Paris gave her the golden apple. From that time the goddesses Hera and Athena were the bitterest enemies of Paris and Troy.

The fairest of all women on earth was Helen, who was already the wife of Menelaus of Sparta, Greece. Under the protection of Aphrodite, Paris sailed to Greece, and while being entertained in the palace of Menelaus, won the love of Helen. Then he carried her away with him to his home, on the Hellespont (the ancient name for the strait now called the Dardanelles).

Manelaus called upon all the kings and princes of Greece to help him to avenge this great wrong. After two years' preparation the Greek fleet set sail for Troy. The Trojans were well prepared for the conflict. King Priam, though too old to take an active part in battle, had gathered immense supplies of provisions and formed alliances with the neighbouring princes and chieftains. The city was protected by mighty walls.

For more than nine years, the Greeks besieged Troy, with varying fortune. Then Achilles, the bravest and the ablest of Greeks, quarelled over a girl, Briseis, with Agamemnon (brother of Menelaus, called in Homer's *Iliad* the king of men, mythical king of Mycenae who was leader of Greek army that sailed for Troy) and refused to take further part in the conflict, until the death of his friend Patroclus caused him to go forth once more to seek vengeance. But after slaying Hector (son of King Priam of Troy), Achilles was himself killed by the god Apollo who had loved Hector and the Greeks were in despair. Then Odysseus (known also a Ulysses), aided by the goddess Athena, devised the famous wooden horse, large enough to contain 100 armed warriors. Helen, for whose sake the dreadful war had been waged, was again in the arms of her husband Menelaus and the war-weary Greeks made ready to return to the wives and children whom they had not seen for 10 years.

The Greek myths and legends, though well-defined, are anacreontic, after the manner of their poet Anacreon: free, convivial, erotic. The active and domineering role played by the goddesses themselves has been of far greater consequence than in most other legends. To start with, the conflict remained confined to supernatural beings. Rivals like Callisto were thrown up in oblivion and Hera got a thousand ships launched to soothen her ego hurt by Aphrodite and when even the mighty Achilles failed, Athena employed her ingenuity and cunningness to put to use the Trojan Horse to satisfy her own vanity. Man initially escaped such upheavels.

According to classical Greek mythology, originally man was androgynous, having the characteristics of both male and female in one individual. He had been complete in himslef. He did not need anything else. He was self-satisfied. This self-centredness eventually became a threat to the gods and especially to Zeus. When man had fallen into a brutish state and the wrath of Zeus was aroused against them, Prometheus (one of the Titans) came forward as their champion. He taught them the useful arts, and stole fire from heavens for their use. Zeus then caused a woman to be made from clay to bring trouble to mankind.

Pandora was the first woman on earth. She was fashioned by Hephaestus (Vulcan, son of Zeus and Hera, god of fire and blacksmith of the gods), and each of the other gods conferred some gift, hence her name, which means "all-gifted". Aphrodite gave beauty, Hermes (Mercury), son of Zeus, boldness, self-confidence, cunning and persuation, Athena, feminine accomplishments. Zeus sent her to Prometheus' brother Epimetheus, who gladly accepted her as his wife, though Prometheus had cautioned him against her. Pandora brought with her a jar or box in which were all men's ills and troubles, and which she had been warned not to open. When she opened it, they escaped and spread over the whole earth, Hope alone remaining. A later story has it that the jar contained all blessings, which would have been preserved for mankind had not Pandora opened it and allowed all but Hope to escape.

Whatever be the version, the First Lady Pandora did not know what the box contained. Little did the latter day Pandora know that despite being well-armed with all the artifice bestowed upon her, her companion in few cases would not remain dormant when denied her presence and world go hell for leather for any stop-gap arrangement in her absence even to the depths of the Dead Sea landing up with the Apple of Sodom, fair to look at but without any substance.

It was left to latter psycho-analysts to study the abomination which they thought was the consequence of repression. According to them, there are three main groups of positive sexuality, "A pronounced biologically normal trend which expresses itself in heterosexual desire; a pronounced abnormal trend which must lead to homosexual desire; and a pathologically unstable trend which may lead to both heterosexual and homosexual desires under the influence of early repressions and environmental conditions which may influence the normal endocrine factors and activate the abnormal. Even the most emotionally normal and balanced human beings will have recourse to some kinds of sexual equivalents or substitute gratifications under prolonged and complete deprivation of normal satisfaction".[1] Many become masturbators by necessity, as in prisons, little realising that this surrender to passion can bring about a change in the form of genitals and, apart from this local anatomical influence, can have serious consequences on the whole organism. Others develop homosexual habits as in ships.

Justifications can be offered for any vice. Unless one is guided by innate moral teachings, deprivation of normal life can make some human minds run amuck. Vindication couched in however masterly a language cannot hide the regret that the inner self throws up. Let us see how Lawrence of Arabia, lord in many fields, justifies the phenomenon.

"Some of the evil of my tale may have been inherent in our

---

[1] *Woman*, op.cit., vol. i, pp. 133-136

circusmstances. For years we lived under the indifferent heaven... The men were young and sturdy; and hot blood unconsciously claimed a right in them and tormented their bodies with strange longings... The public women of the rare settlements we encountered in our months of wanderings would have been nothing to our numbers, even had their raddled meat been palatable to a man of healthy parts. In horror of such sordid commerce our youth began indifferently to slake one another's few needs in their own clean bodies... Several thirsting to punish appetites they could not wholly prevent, took a savage pride in degrading the body, and offered themselves, fiercely in any habit which promised physical pain or filth."[2]

Each indulgence inevitably generates its own revulsion. Man's bestiality boomeranged on himself and some women in revolt against neglect, suppression or humiliation also, developed an aversion to normal relationship. It is not that only those women who were herded together like goats in a harem fell a victim to this abnormality. Some found that relationship within their own gender was less beastly and that it allowed them to assert that they could survive within their own milieu and repay back the floundering male with the same counterfeit coin. Let us also see this vexatious problem from another angle that has led to its escalation outside India. It is the parents' desire, universally, that a young girl gets married off. In Western society, if a girl of 13 or 14 does not find 'dates', i.e., boys who take her out, the parents start worrying. It is considered that there is something wrong with the girl. She is made to feel as if she is abnormal, physically or mentally or both. Emotional break-downs and rising lesbianism are the outcome of this socio-cultural norm. Luckily there are hardly any lesbians in India so far because equally scarcely there are any spinsters.

Be it said to the credit of the white man, that he has done research in every eccentrictity. "Hirschfeld has investigated and enumerated homosexual methods of physical gratification. He finds

---

[2] T.E. Lawrence of Arabia, *Seven Pillars of Wisdom*, Jonathen Cape Ltd., London, Jan. 46, p.27.

four methods between homosexual men (a) Manual or digital which according to Hirschfeld is preferred by forty per cent; (b) Oral, preferred by another forty per cent (c) Femoral, preferred by about twelve per cent and (d) Anal, the favourite methods of only eight per cent, although this particular action is generally considered typical of male homosexuality or even identified therewith."[3] Among homosexual women he has noted near similar abnormalities without statistics.

Let us see how the synod of the Church of England debated homosexuality in November, 1987:

> "Behind the general discussion lay the practical issue whether homosexuals could serve as clergymen...It has been estimated that possibly a third of the clergy is homosexual..."

Before the 564 members of the synod was a motion affirming that "fornication, adultery and homosexual acts are sinful in all circumstances" and that Christian leaders should be "exemplary in all spheres of morality, including sexual morality, as a condition of office."

"In the debate, Dr. Robert Runcie, Archbishop of Canterbury and the primate of the church, summarised the dilemma. 'I do not deny, and cannot, that homosexual acts are condemned in the Biblical and Christian tradition', but then continued, 'in the face of much cruel prejudice I want to insist that to be homosexual by nature is to be a full human being' (sic). As to the nub of the matter, he concluded that the behaviour of clergymen in this area ought not be judged by their peers, but was best left 'to their fathers in God'.

"Opposed to the motion which would have led to the expulsion of homosexual clerics was an amendment presented by a spokesman for the lesbian and gay Christian movement. This

---

[3] M.Hirschfeld – *Die Homosexulitat des Mannes u.d. Weibes*, Berlin, 1914; *Woman*, op.cit., vol. i, p. 136.

on the Church to encourage 'stability, commitment and permanence in all human relationships', in effect accepting homosexuality so long as it was not practised promiscuously... by an overwhelming majority, the general synod accepted another amended resolution...it expressed disapproval of 'homosexual genital acts' but, in the scale of sinfulness, placed them in a less heinous category than fornication and adultery. The approved resolution did not call for any action to be taken against homosexuals who 'are to be met by a call to repentance and the exercise of compassion...." [4]

No one, I suppose, has so far made an open announcement, ex Cathedra in the Papal church, that homosexuality is lower in the order of abominations than fornication or adultery. Our ancients in India were not oblivious of different forms of abnormal acts. "The religious texts, especially the *Dharmashastras*, strongly condemn unconventional sexual desires. The sexual act is commanded to be performed only through the vulva. Vashistha, the law giver, says that whosoever has 'unnatural' intercourse with his wife, his forefathers have to live the month through in his seed. According to another law giver, Mahanirvanat, such a person is to be punished even with death. Boudhyana says that anyone practising such lewdness or any other kind of forbidden sexual intercourse has to bear the sin of a Brahman murder (Meyer 1971). Such cravings are seen as one of the dreadful things making their appearance towards the end of the world. Lesbian love between girls is punished with a heavy fine and the strokes of the whip; and the married woman who thus stains a maid is at once shaved bald, and with two fingers cut off is led on an ass through the city (Manu, VIII). Similarly by homosexual perversion, a person is supposed to lose his caste. (Manu XI). Severe penance is prescribed as atonement for such sins. Thus the most important norm guiding sexual relations between man and woman is that sexual pleasure should always be lawful and normal. This is applicable to woman and man alike". [5]

---

[4] William Frankel, from London, *The Statesman*, 21 Nov., 1987.

[5] Ranjana Kumari, *Female Sexuality in Hinduism*, published for Joint Women's Programme by the Indians Society for Promoting Christian Knowledge, Delhi, 1988, p.17.

Of Hindus, Tavernier observed, "Adultery is very rare among them and as for sodomy, I have never heard it mentioned." [6] Concern and condemnation, however had been expressed earlier over the known oral form, *Auparishtaka* indulged in with women or men or within women and it was directed that it, "should never be done by a learned Brahman, by a minister that carries on the business of a state or by a man of good reputation..."[7] On this, Burton, who translated *Kama Sutra* in 1883 observed, "From the sculptures being found in (Orissa) it would seem that this practice was popular in that part of the country at that time. It does not seem to be so prevalent now in Hindustan, its place perhaps being supplanted by the practice of sodomy introduced since the Muslim period".[8] Can we now hope that our *Shankaracharyas*, *Imams*, Bishops and the *Granthis* would express their views against this perversity which should help restore normalcy in human relationship to some extent?

Having had a look at this heartless harmony in the vacuum, shall we move around to have a look at a low wet land?

---

6 P.N. Chopra, *Some Experiments in Social Reforms in Mediaeval India; The Cultural Heritage of India*, op.cit., vol. ii, p.639.

7 *The Kama Sutra of Vatsyayana*, Sir Richard F. Burton (who also translated *Arabian Nights* in 16 volumes) and F.F. Arbuthnot, Jaico Publishing House, Bombay, 1979, p. 65.

8 *The Kama Sutra*, op. cit., 62.

15

THE DISORDERED OLDEST PROFESSION

It is time to hit the nail straight on its head. According to Freud if the suppression of sexual instincts is prolonged it may lead to sexual neurosis. He has rightly said that neurosis is impossible in normal sexual life. Compulsory neurosis — disordered nervous system —is considered by him as sexophobia which seeks out and pursues all sexual objects and activities in order to denounce and punish. Sexophobiacs get sexual gratification even when they throw dirt on women by remarks or physical demonstration. What else can explain the tragedy at Qutab Minar that led to its closure? The deadly stampede that followed when some hungry lunatics attempted to harass a couple of women in the narrow stairs full of school children. Has any one carried out any research as to who are the greatest sexophobiacs in our country, and why they are worse and more than anywhere else in the world, who play havoc day in and day out making it impossible for any young girl to venture out alone from her house after sunset anywhere in north India?

- Is it the pattern in the villages where ninety per cent of our people, some poorest of the poor live?
- Is it the moneyed class debauching in the night clubs?
- Is it the urban middle class struggling to make their two ends meet?
- Is it the 'cheap Indian labour' anxious to belabour itself to the utmost so that the overtime earnings may feed the overgrown family?

The answer, I suppose, is an emphatic no.

Who then is it? One guess is that it is the element of our idle class driven away from the villages to the *jhuggis* or street pavements in the cities in quest of a better life, who find that the utopia is delusory and react rabidly. Some of them are unregistered coolies at the stations or bus stops, casual labour on daily basis, menials ever-changing-their-masters or part-time road-side hawkers, who get the false satisfaction of being an Amitabh

Bachan when they confidently harass a mute shirt-clad specimen of the *jeuness dorée*. These idle miserly bats normally while away their time in pubic parks in day time and prowl at night yearning for a chance encounter to prove how quick they are on the uptake. A Marilyn Monroe, having been raped at six, could still rise to have her profile pictured all the way down, with all her dresses put away, just having the radio on. What about our girls busted at the age of three in the heart of cities by men driven by sheer savage madness, their paralysed hormones bursting out at the sight of any graspable pair of legs and then murdering the innocent child throwing her body in a dirty *nullah*? Ms. Kiran Bedi, as director of The Narcotics Control Bureau said that in Delhi's *jhuggis*, inhumanly congested slums, three cases of minor girls being raped are reported every fortnight.[1] We know that only few a cases can be reported to the police by these poor. Should it then not be obligatory on our part to remove these dens of all conceivable vices to open spaces? Is it not a must on many humanitarian grounds?

It is not that one has to find a sinecure for only this deprived under-privileged class. What about the so called white collared educated *babus*, third grade salesmen and petty shopkeepers, and even the greying fathers with better means who cannot help shunting into any woman in an overcrowded bus making her pray that the arduous journey gets soon over?

That brings us to the relief provided by the oldest profession known to mankind. The word 'prostitution' is nowdays used as often wrongly as rightly. In many spheres any extra marital intercourse is designated prostitution. That is quite incorrect. A woman, who lives with a man as his concubine, is thus not necessarily a prostitute. Free love and the so called 'liaison' (illicit connections) must likewise be eliminated. The essence of prostitution lies in earning money for a living by offering the body to various men, if and only if, the gain thereby is the first consideration.

---

[1] The Times of India, 4 Aug. 1990

According to a Western school of thought: "Its roots lie rather in antiquity...It is the result of 'a false morality', especially of the struggle for monogamy. Woman herself is not the party least guilty in the matter... because she demands monogamy before everything thus misunderstanding the polygamous nature of the male and driving him to a sexual satisfaction which he can buy... So long as (monogamous) marriage exists, prostitution will exist also and since we cannot eliminate marriage without the abandonment of our civilisation, we cannot eliminate prostitution however much it may be called a necessry evil".[2]

In India for quite some time as in Greece in the days of hatoerism, prostitution was not just an ordeal that any uncouth recipient could go through. Men demanded and found stimulating pleasure in fond intercourse with women, who by their cultivation, refinement of manners, and witty conversation, together with the surrender of their female charms, exercised an irresistible power of attraction over them. Young men were encouraged by elderly friends to learn the art of making love in such surroundings. Many times the fallen ones were called to respectable homes to teach their women-folk all the finesse of coquetry. Earlier in China the flower girls (in flower boats) were the epitome of all beauty, good education and culture and were sought by male youths to complete their own education. Japan's famous *geisha* needs no introduction though some others, less refined were called 'The lotus in the marsh'. They all took up the profession from necessity; 'she has stained her body but not her heart'. Just like the French girls who publicly announced entry into their new vocation by flinging their hats over the windmill; *le Moulin Rouge*!

Later, the profession was developed on a mass scale. In the Crusades, in the army on the march, there were women of the war canteen. In the army of Charles the Bold there were 900 priests and 1600 prostitutes, courtesans hardened enough to become a part of camp followers. Deliberate efforts were made by the Ea India Company to export British prostitutes to India so that the young

---

2 Woman, op.cit., vol. ii, p. 78.

colonialists were not kept starved of white company.

In Islam, one is told, the position was different. In the *Quran Sura* 24 ("the light") the great Mohammed ordered, " A whore and a whore-monger ye shall whip with a hundred strokes..." [3] This may appear to be a harsh edict. However, if one looks at it objectively, it appears only logical. With legal backing and sanction to have four wives, with option to replace any one of them at any time, how could one have authorised polygamy synchronously with prostitution? What excuse, therefore, can there be when one sees open violation in Kuwait, one of the staunchest preservers of the faith today? In 'Friday markets', every Friday being Sunday there, some maid servants mostly from India, Pakistan, Bangladesh, Sri Lanka, Philippines and Thailand, who come for more money are got prepared for the purpose and are just picked up by the *sheikhs* in their limousines for a day's fun, to country houses or may be to their own homes where even the faithful *begums* assist by playing the stereo loud enought to drown any screams of orgy if the object faces more than a single person. Has this limited hours game, ever been objected to by anyone of the faithful? And the ones who volunteer to undergo the weekly *mela* or ordeal happen to be earning enough in normal course anyway. How money and desire for more money makes the horses and the mares move in tandem in the weekly merry-go-round! In the very recent past there was a demonstration by Sri Lankan girls, both those who had aborted and some still pregnant, in front of their embassy in Kuwait demanding a ban on sending of their girls any further to Kuwait. Photographs appeared in European press showing that the girls did not want their sisters to go through the ordeals their masters and the guests thereof had inflicted on them. Indian girsls by nature are trained not to protest but it is a shame that today any girl, howsoever respectful, if dressed in *saree* moves out in Kuwait, she is considered and physically misbehaved with as passable. At what cost do we need foreign exhange ?

In 1984, I was waiting for my plane to take off from the

---

3 Women, op.cit., vol. ii, p. 80.

Saddam airport in Iraq. Iraqi girls of the present generation who have taken to education and western attire give one the satisfaction that a segment of half of humanity which had its feet strangled is now able to put its best foot forward. There now, even the old women do not cover their face with the *burqa* or a nose-cap. The plane was delayed and passengers ordered their lunch in the lounge. Near me on the floor itself squatted a score plus of women fully covered in their burqas from top to toe, disregarding the available sofas. Just a few steps away, unmindful of the din at the airport, was a sole adherent busy in his *namaz*. Prayers over, he sat on a chair and three of the women served him lunch on his table without pushing back their veils during service to their lord. The other women on the floor below held their plates on their legs by one hand, putting the other under the veil, and ate their meals, some of them taking care that the mouth remained invisible. Dark ankles and silver anklets made me wonder where they came from. Some were not that well-trained and could not keep their faces hidden. What one saw were pictures of prolonged withering misery stamped too hard on too early an age. The 'lord', as I found later, in talk with him, was from Hyderabad, a labour supplier catering to domestic needs in Arabia who had brought his flock out as a reward for services rendered there on *ziarat* to visit the sacred place of Karbala in Iraq. The young ones like *la chévre* (the goat) of Moliere had no doubt paid a heavy price for not heeding to the wise counsel of not going beyond the advised parameters. But what about this piggish flesh-trader thriving on account of the once-young now moth-eaten labour taken from Hyderabad for honest work in the promised land who were now left with skins wrinkled as that of sucked mangos, their dark tint not being able to hide the darker circles around eyes sunk deep? Pig-sticking may have become a lost sport in India but do these whoremasters deserve any better than being gored aground to groan in pain for reviving the earlier much cursed Indenture system, in condemnation of which the sanest and the boldest British elements protested so vehemently against their own authorities? A word here on that system:

"The revelations by Mr C.F. Andrews of what he had seen

with his own eyes in Fiji sent a shock of horror through India... he could not imagine that Englishmen would sanction the continuance in a colony of indentured slavery, a form of slavery more inhuman and demoralising than chattel slavery as it existed in British colonies or in southern states of North America. A chattel slave... was bought for life or until his owner sold him again. In either case, good physical treatment was to the owner's interest, since on that depended the value for work or sale, of his property. But in indentured slavery, the conditions are far worse. The coolie is bought through a 'recruiter' — at Rs.45 for man, Rs. 55 for a woman. He is bought for five years only, and during his term his cost must be replaced, and all the possible profit must be made out of him. His strength is to be wrung out of him to the last ounce... That he is a wreck at the end of five years matters not at all... The enslaved man is secured by fraudulent promises, the woman is often kidnapped as are young boys... The kidnapper in Africa of negroes is now hunted down on the high seas; the recruiter in India is licensed... Once in the recruiter's grip and taken to a local depot the woman's face is certainly, the man's almost always, sealed; the woman's character is gone; she has been taken away by a strange man for the night to a place away from her family. Scared and shamed, she is taken before a magistrate; she is registered. From the moment that they... are registered... they are bondsmen. And to make things worse, a boy is minor up to 18 years of age by Indian Law and cannot make a valid contract, but by a special section of the Act of 1908, he may sign away his liberty for five years, signing an agreement to emigrate, when he is only 16... Let us 'agitate, agitate, agitate' until the law is changed...[4]

Were the earlier slave traders any worse than the present day fleshmongers who take their prey out on a contract for two years to Arabia and then try to mitigate their offence by taking their victims on a pilgrimage to Karbala as a recompense? Would Muhammed Iqbal, on seeing this sorry spectacle be still able to compose the hymn, and if he did, which one of these poor damsels be able to sing with him:

---

[4] Annie Besant, The Commonwealth, 16 Feb. 1917.

"Sare Jahan se achha, Hindostan hamara,
Hum bulbulein hain iski, yeh gulsitan hamara"
(Better than the whole Universe, is our Hindostan,
We are its nightingales, this, our endless valley of flowers).

Coming back to the hackneyed subject of the oldest profession, in no field have views changed so essentially from time to time in some civilised countries of Europe as those regarding prostitution. The changes at one time brought out in Europe succeeded in abolishing most of the brothels in order so it is said, to elevate the honour of women. Unlicensed prostitution due to abolition of the brothels had its repercussions. With the relatively strict discipline of the brothels gone and in the absence of hygienic measures came the enormous increase in syphilis. "The consequence was that whole people were tainted not only with syphilis but also with prostitution which caused such endless misery throughout Europe... Thus brothels were again introduced everywhere but a terrible mistake was made. They were no longer public institutions with honourable management but clandestine corners full of alcohol, dirty speculation and shameful exploitation of young women... He who solves the question of prostitution solves the whole sexual questions and how to solve this will shortly be one of the most burning questions which must come before the public"...[5]

Any society, howsoever old, in order to grow has to think of not one but various outlets. Age-old practices should not be wiped off and proven diversions like sports activities, must not be buried. As a digression, let us take our mind just a few decades back. Schools and colleges were limited but most of them had some sports field of some kind where those who cared to spend a healthy evening. Now all cities are developing centrifugally in fresh space. Yet where are the open fields to play on? Even the centuries-old established play-fields in the older cities have become centres of some form of economic activity. Take the case of the various clubs

---

[5] Woman, op.cit., vol. ii, p.106.

with proper ballrooms to dance on. The sheer pleasure of holding a waist line and clasping a hand kept the mind on even keel in rhyme with the best of melodies. These dance floors have now been converted into rummy rooms where bloated bodies are more concerned with quick intake of easy money. The present version of *Raslila* (public dancing) is almost extinct. Thus, deprived of healthy diversions, where do our young folk go? By not finding any time for them and also keeping them away from women, song, dance or games, are we not driving them to drugs?

An Irish saying has it that, "There is nothing so pure as a reformed whore". Yet, one doesn't have to be an old hag to suggest reforms. Let us take a look at the steps taken by Joanna I, Queen of Naples and Countess of Provence, when she founded a house in Avignon. She was then 23. The statutes were still extant, based on report of 1935. The following are extracts :

"(1) On the 8th of August in the year 1347, our good Queen Joanna has permitted a house for young women to be erected in Avignon for the pleasure of the public. She will not (allow) all the courtesans to be spread throughout the town...

"(2) If a girl has once fallen and goes forth to abandon herself again, then shall the bailiff bring her to the house where her future companions in pleasure are assembled...

"(3) A door shall be made through which anyone can enter, but it shall remain locked so that no male person may visit the red marked girls without persmission of the female Superintendent, who is to be chosen anew every year by the Town Council. The Superintendent... shall warn the young people seriously to make no uproar or torment the girls.

(4) It is the will of the Queen that every Saturday the Superintendent and a surgeon chosen by the Council shall examine each girl, and if one of them is found infected by an evil arisig from coitus, then she shall be separated from the others and put in a separate room and the infection of

the young be prevented."[6]

There was a small queen who gave some thought to this labyrinthine problem six centuries back. The high ecclesiastical authorities in Europe eventually remembered an old dictum of St. Thomas which says: "Prostitution in towns is like the cesspool (a pool or hollow in which filthy water collects) in the palace; take away the cesspool and the palace will become an unclean and evil smelling place".[7] In our context by abolishing these private houses, say in Delhi, we have dispersed the show to each colony and not only forced the enterpreneurs to be in the clutches of the blood sucking *dadas* but also allowed ingress of the germ in fresher fields where innocent minds may succumb to temptation of easy money, with little likelihood of regaining themselves. Perhaps we could learn something from others and when the present altruistic feminist approach is past, may draw correct conclusios.

Anthropologists from earlier times "have often attempted to explain satisfactorily the oft-stated fact that professional prostitutes almost always try to return to their vocation even if the possiblity is offered to them of being able to lead a carefree and regular life instead of this existence full of shame, persecution, care and privation."[8] Those who happen to be at the helm of affairs might benefit from this and remember that no *Nari Niketans*, i.e. State houses for destitute women, can serve the dual purpose of providing an alternative vocation to these women of easy virtue as well as give shelter to other women needing protection. These *Niketans* have become houses of evil under different guises and provide a sorry spectacle of State exploitation. What else can one conclude when one sees a report:

"The Supreme Court today admitted a letter alleging exploitation of inmates of the house for destitute women in Patna and issued notices to the Bihar Government, the district judge of

---

6 Woman, op.cit., vol. ii, p.97.
7 Woman, op.cit., vol. ii, p.97.
8 Woman, op.cit., vol. ii, p.110.

Patna and the Caretaker of the home... The inmates numbering 100 had to satisfy the needs of the staff and the management of the care-home, alleged the written petition. Even outsiders and anti-social elements visited the home. Some of the inmates are sent out side the care-home campus to extract money from customers. If they tried to resist the 'offence' they were brutally assaulted, ravished and starved for a day or two... at least 25 inmates had 'gone mad'... Megha Verma, an MA student, also went mad after she was lodged at the home..." [9] But why talk of backward Bihar of 1987 when in the cosmopolitan city of New Delhi, Lt. Governor Arjan Singh had to assure a women's delegation in 1990 that he would "personally look into the affairs of *Nari Niketan* following their allegations that *Nari Niketan*/Women Wards of Tihar jail (Delhi) are working as dens and women inmates at these places are compelled to get involved in immoral acts." [10]

Perhaps the answer is to let the oldest profession in the world survive in the joint sector — a mixed sector wherein the State directly assists, controls and protects the workers and helps them manage their show themselves in a clean manner rather than allow touter Shylocks drain the last drop of blood of the vendors and suck the hopping clowns. The State should also ensure that no one is forced to continue to live a life full of shame; punish those who entice others to join this profession and rescue those who earnestly desire to get out of it. Those who are keen to observe all the Draconian laws on these fallen women should not ignore Manu's guidance, "Three things do not become impure — women, gems and water." [11] Therefore, these fallen sisters should be helped to regain themsleves rather than be condemned to live a perpetual viral life.

Yet, we cannot bring down the curtain in the hope that prostitution would be a panacea of all evils and that it would wipe off sexual neurosis like a magic wand. Another violation of the

---

9 The Times of India, 18 Nov 1987.

10 The Hindustan Times, 16 Sep 1990.

11 Manu III. 32. 60-62.

marriage-bed withholds man and wife from keeping their body and soul together and, in this advanced jugglery, one cannot blame one participant more than the other. Many times, false passions lurking behind the stage-door broil up to such an extent that they throw up the whole cast as dismal shadows on the stage. We may as well have a look at this theatrical piece.

16

ADULTERY AND THE WRATH OF THE OVERLORDS

The story of Creation is as fascinating as any that can be found in any scripture. The Bible gives an account of Adam and Eve in the Garden of Eden and it needed a John Milton (1608-74) to describe in unmatched magnificence the great events which led to their expulsion from Paradise. Satan, sitting on the Tree of Life in the Garden — the forbidden Tree— like a bird of prey looked out upon the wonders of the place, and the newly created parents of the human race —

"Two of far nobler sight, erect and tall
God-like erect, with native honour clad,
In naked majesty...
For contemplation he and valour formed,
For softness she and sweet attractive grace...
He for God only, she for God in him."[1]

One can perceive the delicate difference that God intended to have between the two since their inception. Perhaps He realised that the soft and sweet Eve, without the backing of her Adam, would be easily beguiled by Satan to look for short pleasures. Angel Raphael was sent to warn Adam against the wiles of the Evil One but the Fiend's work to seduce the new race of Man to rise in revolt against God had already been done. When the forbidden fruit from the Tree of Knowledge was eaten against the express command —

"Sky loured, and muttering thunder, some sad drops
Wept at completing of the mortal skin,
...They swim in mirth and fancy that they feel
Divinity within them breeding wings
Wherewith to scorn the Earth..."[2]

---

[1] *Paradise Lost*, Book IV.
[2] *Paradise Lost*, Book IX.

But soon their high sprits drooped and they quarelled. Becoming ashamed of their nakedness they put on girdles of leaves and in repentance hid themselves in the Garden. God became angry with Adam for disobeying Him but Adam, with his inborn chivalry made the excuse, "The woman whom thou gavest to be with me, she gave me of the tree and I did eat."God in His judgment became biased and the differences between the two sexes became more pronounced. He told the woman, " I will greatly multiply thy sorrow and thy conception: in sorrow thou shalt bring forth children and thy desire shall be to thy husband, and he shall rule over thee". [3] Adam was condemned to till the ground in the sweat of his brow. Both Adam and Eve fell prostrate on the spot where God had judged them and begged pardon "with tears watering the ground". God accepted their repentance and consented to the ultimate redemption of the race but decreed that they must leave Paradise. Be it said to the credit of Adam and Eve that on their departure:

"Some natural tears they dropped but wiped them soon;
The world was all before them, where to choose
Their place of rest and Providence their guide
They, hand in hand, with wandering steps and slow,
Through Eden took their solitary way". [4]

It was a bold resolve to seek new pastures but it was not the last that they heard of Satan who was not content to see them move hand in hand and remain together. God in His benignity had made human beings His choicest creation. He also, inter se, had made Adam a little different from Eve by giving him better brawn if not perhaps brain. As a recompense, in his gractious mood while fashioning her from Adam's rib, He bestowed beauty in abundance on the fair one. It is this contrast in the gifts apportioned which Satan was to exploit later to the full to sow the seeds of discord between the two. Adam is incited to take full advantage of his

---

[3] *Gen.* 3:16.

[4] *Paradise Lost*, Book IX.

(Photo Courtesy Mr. M. L. Garg)

physical potency, to prowl around and maltreat woman. Eve is induced to let her beauty be appreciated by more than one admirer and forget to see her God in a solitary figure. An when either of them is unable to retain what is granted to them in ample measure due to over indulgence, the stage is all set for them to go through infernal regions here on Earth itself.

Now in a short article, *The Love Bug*, published underneath a fine piece of sculpture, the Indian youth is being advised not to consider sex outside marriage as sinful. All the motivation is being provided by the sculptured prince's casual caressing of the charming princess' delicate bosom of firm fullness having orbicular contours and bold swelling erect nipples, reminding one of the beauty which in the words of Firdausi (A.D. 960), " the breeze dare not touch but longs from afar".

It is perhaps not realised that one of the greatest gifts of God, by which He has shown singular partiality to mankind, is the provision of charming breasts to our females which not only are personification of feminine beauty but also a source of sensual pleasure both to her and her companion.

> *"Téton, téton, charmant qui jamais ne repose,*
> *Vous semblez inviter la main a vous presser,*
> *L'oeil a vous contempler, la bouchę a vous baiser."*
> (Bosom, charming bosom which never rests,
> you seem to invite the hand to press you,
> The eye to behold you, the mouth to kiss you).

Yet such are the laws of nature that as time passes the same exuberant bosoms sag. By her make-up, a woman wears out earlier due to accompaniments of menstruation, conception and eventual menopause, which in some cases drives her companion away. If this alone is the cause, perhaps the outclassed woman would herself gracefully retire from the race. No such stipulation is proposed now and all one can see in an exhortion to open fornication and lewdness where everything is held in common resulting in what may be termed sexual communism: "from each according to his capacity, to each according to his need."

Instead of getting involved in any dialectics, we should also face the fact that woman with all her innocence has not been unaware of her inbuilt power to animate even the most hardened puritan. Nor could this knowlege remain hidden from Indra, lord of *devtas*, the heavenly gods. Had it been so, when he was losing all battles against the royal sage Vishwamitra and was finding his own throne in the doldrums, he would not have taken recourse to send the bewitching temptress Menaka to lure and entice the high celibatarian away from his prayers. And Menaka, the greatest *apsara* (celestial dancer), would not have embarked on the venture if it was to be fruitless.

Manu had much earlier cautioned men, "It is the nature of woman to seduce men; for that reason the wise are never unguarded" [5] Little could Manu perceive that man would allow himself to be so overwhelmed by his own passion that his additional mistress would wield all the privileges of authority without any responsibility. Worse would follow, when the injured vanity of his life-mate would recoil upon him reducing him to a cuckold, burdened with all the responsibility but without any authority over either his old companion or the new *femme fatale*.

At this stage we must clearly understand that the term adultery is restricted to voluntary union of a married person with one who is not his or her lawful spouse. Both man and woman who indulge in it are equally involved and the fault should not be placed on woman alone, or more on her.

Not that this strange malady escaped the attention of the ancients. The *Mahabharata* does refer to traces of promiscuity in marital relations in ancient India, when it narrates how Svetaketu enjoined that there should be no laxity in conjugal relation. The *Rig-veda* also occasionallly refers to the woman without guardians going astrary. But the perusal of the marriage hymn, shows that the sanctity of the

---

5 *Rigveda*, X. 85.

institution of marriage had already been recognised by the society, and the lapses, which one noticed here and there were as much as were difficult to eliminate in all times and in all through life. Being aware of this reality, certain heavy penances were ordained for both men and women but the extreme penance was prescribed for men only for certain forms of adultery. "According to Visnu followed among others by Sulapani, all guilty of *atipatakas* (incest with mother, daughter and daughter-in-law) should enter a burning fire, and no other penance exists for them ".[6] In the course of our social development there was hardly any need for such injunctions as conjugal faithfulness became an inherent part of our life, its infringement being hardly resorted to by married women. Akbar held a high opinion of the chastity of Hindu women, who, in spite of being sometimes neglected, were "flaming torches of love and fellowship." [7] Jahangir admired the fidelity of Hindu women who would not allow "the hand of any unlawful person touch the skirt of their chastity, and would rather perish in flames."[8]

In the European concept, " as depicted in the old French epics, marriage is a matter of mutual convenience and protection rather than love. Women preserved their affection for former admirers and had no hesitation in loving outside marriage if they were so inclined or if the occasions were propitious. Adultery on the part of the man is not mentioned in these poems" [9] In Italy things went a step further. "Cicisbeism was once so generally known that no married Italian lady, although probably quite wrongfully, used to be imagined without such a companion", [10] her *cavaliere servente*, her gallant Cicisbeo. The concept was and is of free play, a wife formally bearing a name not bothered to bear the name's offsprings, the crow of a husband providing the nest for the unknown male cuckoo's effort and feeling no worse for it. The

---

6 D.C. Bhattacharya, *Penances and Vows*, *The Cultural Heritage of India*, op.cit., vol.ii, p.387.

7 *Akbarnama* III, p.372; *The Cultural Heritage of India*, op.cit., vol.ii, p.639.

8 *Tuzuk-i-Jahangiri*, op.cit., II, p. 268; *The Cultural Heritage of India*, op.cit., vol. ii, p. 639.

9 *Woman*, op.cit., vol. i, p. 533.

10 *Woman*, op.cit., vol. ii, p. 248.

European concept even earlier did clarify, "In any case, there can be no question of adultery where the husbands themselves, whether from some exaggerated feeling of hospitality or from some desire to gain, resign their wives to other men for sexual intercourse, for *volenti non fit injuria.* It is the wrong done to the husband granted to him alone which is always what we must consider when we are supposed to be speaking of an infringement of marriage..." [11] Today unless there is an open abuse of marital tie-up, making it a talking point leading to embarrassment, many Europeans both men and women, do not bother to waste their time on this subject.

In some societies there are strong reactions against adultery yet must repercussions go beyond any civilised compassion without even seeing the merits of the case? One therefore cannot fail to react when one reads the operational portion of a jaudgment passed by a court in Karachi, Pakistan, in 1987 exercising its power under the *Hudood* Ordinance against adultery: "The couple shall be buried up to their necks and stoned to death in public". The report says, "Shahida Parveen, 26, and her husband Mohammed Sarwar, 36, are awaiting the execution of the sentence in a jail... Shahida was married at 13 years age to a 40 years old man, Khushi Mohammad Khan, against her will. Later, she separated from him and married Mohammad Sarwar and was not living clandestinely with him when the priests in the male dominated society refused to grant *Khula* or *Faksh* to her". [12] Four years earlier, a trial court had subjected a 20 year old blind girl, Safia bibi, who was subjected to *Zina-bil-jabr* (rape) by her employer Maqsood Ahmed. He was acquitted for want of evidence but she was sentenced to three years rigorous imprisonment and 15 lashes: which was luckily commuted by Shariat Court. Allah be praised that experts on Muslim laws both in India and Pakistan have opined that the infliction of *hadd* by the Karachi judge was "mindless and cruel".

The *Hudood* Ordinance passed in 1980 is considered by some

---

[11] Woman, op.cit., vol. ii, p. 238.

[12] *The Times of India*, 14 Dec., 1987.

to equate adultery with rape. Thousands of women, raped and then accused of adultery are reported to be languishing in the jails in Pakistan. The result it that women do not report a rape lest they are accused of adultery, stoned to death or jailed. Unfortunately, some persons, in order to retain their power take steps which denigrate women.. As Annes Jung has brought out after her recent visit to Pakistan, "The brand of Islam promulgamated by Zia, more orthodox than that in Wahabi Saudi Arabia, tended to concentrate on those social aspects that impinge on women — marriage, family, divorce, a dress code". [13] These die-hards forget that the advent of Islam had caused improvement in social interactions prevalent at that time. But can one say that what was done fourteen centuries ago to counter malpractices in a particular region is enough to meet the requirements of today when Islam is prevalent worldwide? Some reforms have already been adopted in Turkey, Syria, Jordan and Iraq. It is not that the process did not agitate the minds of a few Muslims in India. Iqbal, a very staunch follower of the faith, expressed his opinion, "The claim of the present generation of Muslim liberals to reinterpret the foundational legal principles, in the light of their own experience and altered conditions of modern life is, in my opinion, perfectly justified. The teaching of the *Quran* that the life is a process of progressive creation necessitates that each generation guided but unhampered by the work of its predecessors should be permitted to solve its own problems". [14] One hopes in the light of these words that the notorious *Hudood* Ordinance passed in 1980 would be repealed and some other outmoded misinterpreted injunctions modified to conform to altered environment. It is time also for the Indian Muslims themselves to ponder alone whether the status of women in their society needs improvement. No one else should speak on the subject lest it be misunderstood as uncalled for interference and the resultant backlash may deny our Muslim women chance to live better.

---

[13] *The Times of India*, 6 May 1990.

[14] Dr Sir Muhammed Iqbal, *The Reconstruction of Religious Thought in Islam*, Lahore, p. 168.

Whatever may be the place accorded to women in different religions or regions in India, it is sad to say that today except possibly for the Parsees, there is one common denominator that governs our women's life. Whether Hindu, Muslim or Christian, the Indian woman is required to be in reality an embodiment of self-sacrifice, self-effacement and suffering. A very noble image that has perhaps saved many a marriage but then, would our women continue to pay the heavy cost? The abomination of adultery, galloping in some societies, has not yet been seen in an open polo ground in our milieu. Notwithstanding this, the present day educated wife is not willing to accept what the great Tulsidas, himself a gallant Casanova before he earned his sainthood, had pronounced in the sixteenth century:

Dhol, ganwar, shudra, pashu, nari,
Sakal tadna ke adhikari

(A tambour, an illiterate, person of the lowest fourth caste, an animal and a woman, all of them deserve to be scolded.)

Today, more than ever before, our women are getting exposed to outside influence, becoming aware of their rights, and nothing offends them more than their injued vanity.As time passes they are bound to meet someone who is more captivating or who can give the satisfaction of having taken a revenge. Are we to wander around as slaves of temptation drifting apart with every change in the direction of the wind or are we to sail along merrily in the marital confluence withstanding all storms?

17

THE CONJUGAL BLISS

We will now take a look at the most controversial views expressed by Mr. Sathe that marriage is an institution created by man for social stability and physical union, coming together, has nothing to do with institutionalising. The question arises, is marriage meant only to keep up the facade of social order? Is it a commercial deal or a communion of souls, minds and bodies? Whether it is a contract or sacrament, till what limits can the breaches be permitted?

Before we discuss this matter, it would be worthwhile to consider whether the two sexes ae equal in every field or complementary. The orthodox view was expressed by Virchow, "Putting the two sexes on equal footing should not be attempted on intellectual and physical grounds, for all the differences ordained in the two sexes must remain. Complete emancipation would lead to the dissoultion of the family and to children being brought up by he State, a condition to be found at the lowest level of human civilisation."[1] Even in their priorities, Charles Darwin brought out the difference that, "Women would generally choose not merely the handsomest man, according to their standard of taste, but those who were at the same time best able to defend and support them. Moreover the more vigorous men would seek and obtain the more attractive women".[2] However, in this tussle, whereas woman was clear in her mind and remained contented with basic security, man himself was at a loss in his search because there is no absolute and final judgment in the matter of personal beauty. Alongside the difference in priorities and personal preferences there was new awakening in the West. The thought emerged, much against earlier Christian teaching, that "there is great linguistic absurdity especially with regard to the combination of the concept of 'love and marriage' which have really little to do with each other. Love is, as

---

[1] *Woman*, op.cit., vol. i. p.123.

[2] *Essai sur L'inégalité des races humaines*, Paris, 1853; Woman, op.cit., vol. i, p. 162.

we have said, an endocrinic process (pouring its secretions directly into blood or lymph); marriage is an economic creation, the chemical processes leading to erotic sensibility are not absolutely necessry to it but an economic basis is essential... The desire of our youth to marry for love alone is a lamentable error which is dying out... It is false to conclude: This marriage is a lasting one, that is to say, the husband and wife will 'love' each other for ever. Absolutely false too is the idea that there is lasting erotic impulse which supports the theory of monogamy..." [3] What a lovely concept! Marriage having no everlasting foundtions of love, happiness and sex which have to be fished from different streams.

In India, monogamy was the usual rule, but polygamy was permitted and practised by the rich and the ruling classes. Polyandry, though heard of, was unknown. Marriage was regarded as a religious ritual which enjoined the husband to regard his wife as a god-given gift. Manu thus extols the house-holder: "Just as every creature lives by air, so the orders of life exist by the support of the householder ;[4] a wife is the main source of *dharma*, *artha* and *kama* and so an unmarried person, irrespective of the *varna* (caste) to which he belongs, is unfit for the disharge of his duties". [5]

The above formulae contain all the essentials of domestic felicity. In our context, marriage is considered not only essential but a permanent union and not a temporary contract. It is not a licence for indulgence but a human institution aiming at totality in conjugal life, elevating the homogeneity between the couple to a spiritual level.

The eight forms of marriage recognised in the scriptures [6] and listed in ascending order of merit are *paisaca*, *rakasa*, *gandarva*, *asura*, *prajapatya*, *arsa*, *daiva* and *brahma*, and these may be viewed

---

[3] *Woman*, op.cit., vol.ii, p. 159.

[4] Manu III.77.

[5] Yaj., I. 51.

[6] Manu III. 24.

as fraudulent, forcible (by abduction), romantic, commercial, racial, austere, sacrificial and spiritual marriage respectively. The last four are approved religiously (*prasasta*) but the first four are not (*aprasasta*). In the case of approved marriages, the sacrament is a condition precedent, while in the case of the unapproved one, it may be performed after the marriage.The main point to remember is that whatever may have been the means employed to gain a companion, once a union was consummated, the end result was given sanctity.

It is surprising that our ancients did not add a ninth form; the trial marriages of Europe, the peculiar custom of a couple living a regular life of sexual association, sometimes even for several years, the marriage being concluded only if during the trial period the financé succeeded in making his intended bride pregnant. If there was no impregnation it was presumed that the two people were incompatible and they left each other. In 1887, G.V. Bunsen reported the existence of trial period in Yorkshire. The solemn words of the financé on entering upon such a trial relationship run thus "If thee tak, I tak thee" (that is, if thou dost conceive, then I will take thee)." [7] Even this system had certain social sanctions for the abandonment of the girl after she became pregnant was most severely punished by the neighbours. Not infrequently the girl found incompatible with one, found a fresh suitor who went through a new trial period with her.

These days some Europeans have simplified the matter. In order to get rid of the stigma of polygamy or polyandry, they change their partners as fast as one takes up another job for better prospects. Economically we may be backward now but we are not people with closed minds and have a fair inception of what the future beholds if we follow suit. As regards experience, we must take benefit from what the great German Iron Chancellor Bismark said, "Fools learn from their own experience, I prefer to learn from others." Marriage is too serious a matter to be subjected to and be settled only by repeated trial and error. We might, therefore, have a

---

[7] ***Woman***, op.cit., vol.ii, p.218.

look at the latest report on women and love in America by the feminist Ms. Shere Hite who in the *Hite Report* reveals :-

- "70 per cent of women married five years or more are having extra matrimonial affairs, although most of them believe in monogamy.

- 87 per cent say their friendship with other women are emotionally closer than their love relationship with men.

- Only 13 per cent of women married more than two years are 'in love' with their husband.

- 84 per cent of women are unsatisfied emotionally with their relationships".[8]

My dear Indian sisters, the situation is nowhere so ghastly in our country to provoke a corresponding *Hite Report.* You should therefore be in no haste to pick up a mate on a first come first served basis. You may meet a man who projects an image which meets most of your aspirations set in your mind for an ideal partner yet the perfection projected by the beauish boy may only prove to be delusory imagination and not provide the safeguard of a buoy. With parental support still available plenteously, why should you embark only on your own in search of a suitable mate and in the bargain, as happens with many European girls, meet all and sundry in the hope of being able to find one who you consider may foot the bill? Many times in the effort, instead of catching the big fish you may get tied up with a shark. Why not face reality? We are not a newly established society with that open a mind that an unwed mother can rear up and display with pride her produce of pleasure. Even if we press on regardless, it will take us a long time before we allow a Willy Brandt — who was brave enough to acknowlege that he was a bastard and yet retained his chancellorship of Western Germany — to become our President. By all means snap the family cords if you find that ulterior motives are pushing you down the

---

8 Shere Hite, *Women and Love*, Oct 87.

the inferno. Just walk out in rebellion for He who gives life also sustains it. Manu advised, " A girl may remain a spinster rather than her father shall give her in marriage to a worthless man." [9] If the situation is not so desperate, why jump in the fray unguided.? But, to borrow again from Manu, "If within three years of attaining age, her father is not able to find her a suitable husband, she might herself seek one." [10] So if you find that due to any reason your father is unable to make a headway and you on your own have found a suitable companion and made a commitment, stand by it. However, in your quest for the Everest, do not become too reluctant a debutante, for many times those who are too choosy, stand and wait for so long as to miss the bus.

The sum total is that we should not reject out of hand the marital way of life that has seen us through the ages, that has survived all the vicissitudes, that has withstood untold onslaughts. Imitation of cultures that were nearly nomadic when we had built the Iron Pillar which bears an inscription of Chandragupta II, Vikramaditya dated A.D. 413 and whose remaining rust-proof for ages continues to baffle Western scientists till today, will not help us. We can ill afford to throw to the winds our great institution of marriage. Those who had discarded it hit the vodka so hard that they are now reverting back to it.

It is not that the wise in the West have not been aware of this folly. One does not have to be a Shavian to appreciate the wit, sarcasm and clarity of GBS who pronounced, "There is no subject on which more dangerous nonsense is talked and thought than marriage... Now most laws are, and laws ought to be, stronger than the strongest individual. Certainly the marriage law is. The only people who successfully evade it are those who actually avail themselves of its shelter by pretending to be married when they are not, and by Bohemians who have no position to lose and no career to be closed. In every other case open violation of the marriage laws means either downright ruin or such invonvenience and disablement as a prudent man or woman would get married ten

---

[9] Manu, IX.89.

[10] Manu, IX.90.

times over rather than face. And these disablements and inconveniences are not even the price of freedom; for as Brieus has shown so convincingly in les Hannetons, an avowedly illicit union is often found in practice to be as tyranical and as hard to escape from as the worst legal one... Marriage remains practically inevitable; and the sooner we acknowledge this, the sooner we shall set to work to make it decent and reasonable". [11]

But a genius like Shaw is a rare exception to the rule; little read, less understood and least followed. While accepting the requirement of conjugal bliss, the more vibrant opinion makers have led the Western society to a stage of sexual euphoria and things have moved so fast that instead of being told not to marry a stranger in a hurry, their youth have to be advised by such renowned 'sexperts' like Dr. Paul Pearsall, "Never divorce someone you don't know". [12]

Mahatma Gandhi advised, "We must not be entrapped by false analogies. ... What may be therefore true of Europe is not necessarily true of India. We know too, that each nation has its own characteristics and individuality. India has her own; and if we are to find a true solution for many of her ills, we shall have to take all the idiosyncrasies of her constitution into account and then prescribe a remedy... India has stood many a storm. Each has left its own indelible mark, it is true, but she has dauntlessly maintained her individuality. India is one of the few nations of the earth which have witnessed the fall of many civilisations, herself remaining scratchless... she has hitherto shown an inherent capacity for purging herself of error and superstition".[13] It is for us now to concentrate our efforts to eradicate evils like dowry, *Sati* and child marriages rather than add to our miseries by throwing overboard the basic union of the family.

---

[11] George Bernard Shaw, *Getting Married*, Constable and Coy. Ltd., London, 1927, p.109.

[12] *Super marital sex: Loving for life*, Edbury Press, London, 1987.

[13] Gandhi, M.K., *Economics of Khadi*, Navajivan Press Ahmedabad, 1941, p. 134.

18

CHILD MARRIAGES, FEMALE INFANTICIDE AND SPINSTERS

At this stage we should have a look at the institution of child marriages, one of the curses that still afflicts us though other people have got rid of the ordeal sometimes earlier. Furnivall's acount of sixteenth century[1] proves the common occurrence of child marriages in the whole of England at that time apart from giving many an interesting contribution to the history of morals of that period. Research work carried out by a number of Europeans clearly brings out that in many parts of Europe girls were married at the young ages of 12 in Spain and 12th or 13th year in Greece.[2] Napoleon I (1769-1821) postponed the marriages of girls from 13 to 15 years and that of young men from 15 to 18 for, it was asserted that except for a few, marriage at 13 or 14 was accompanied by overwhelming injurious consequences. In Great Britain (excluding Northern Ireland) a measure was passed as late as in 1929 declaring void marriages between persons of either sex who were not 16 years of age. This measure did not in Scotland affect any right or capacity of legitimation *per subsequence matriminio.*[3] In Arabia, wc arc told, all Mohammedans were permitted to enter into matrimony at 10 years of age.[4] The Arab women were said to mature earlier than those who lived in Africa. J. Burce found that, "Men on the African coast of the gulf of Arabia prefer Abyssinian girls whom they purchased with money to the beautiful Arabian women, because the former go on bearing children longer whereas an Arab woman gives birth to childran even in her eleventh year but ceases child-bearing when she is

---

1 F.J. Furnivall, *Child Marriages in the Diocese of Charter*, London, 1897; *Woman*, op.cit., vol.ii, p.130.

2 Virey, *Journal Universel des Sciences*, 1816; *Woman*, op.cit., vol.ii, p.231.

3 *Woman*, op.cit., vol. ii, p.232.

4 *Woman*, op.cit., vol.ii, p.236.

about 20."[5]

In India, Brainerd Ryder[6] states that he would never be able to describe the grief he felt when he saw these half-developed wives with their expression of hopeless suffering, their arms and legs as those of a skeleton, and saw how they walked at the prescribed distance behind their husbands with never a smile on their faces. At 16 years of age, the wives were not as big, as strong and as well-developed as most girls of Europe of 10 and 11. A Hindu girl of 10 resembled 5 or 6 year-old European children. The custom of child marriages admitted of many Hindu wives becoming mother at 14 and bringing a dozen or more underdeveloped, sickly children into the world. An infuriated Annie Besant cried in the wilderness: "The indecency, the outrage of such marriages are invisible to men and women blinded by evil custom, hypnotised by habit. These helpless victims, sold into slavery by their own fathers to pruchased husbands, is it possible that India shall become free so long as this child-slavery remains, and a Hindu girl is, as a Hindu lately said, without apparently any sense of shame, a chattel?"[7] The Hindus may justify that it was a protective measure against the Muslim invaders who would not usually carry off married women.[8] But do we realise what unspeakable horrors such words as 'infant-marriage', 'baby-wife', 'girl-mother' and 'virgin-widow' brought on our womanhood? Though a long time has elapsed since these words were coined up and tremendous improvement has taken place, yet child marriages continue particularly amongst the rural folk. Despite all laws, we are rising on the wave of population explosion. When we move in the 21st century we will be leaving even China behind in population. We are also facing the unhappy corollary where birth control and advanced age of marriage are reducing to a great extent

---

[5] *Travels to discover the source of the Nile*, Edinburgh, 1790, III, p.349; *Woman*, op.cit., vol.ii, p.236.

[6] *The Little Wives of India*, Melbourne, 1892, *Woman*, op.cit., vol.ii, p.135.

[7] *The Birth of New India*, p.161.

[8] Cf. Will Durant, *Our Oriental Heritage*, Simon and Schuster, New York, 1942, pp.489-90.

the percentage of our intelligentia who alone are taking the required steps. Another attendant scourge: earlier, among the Hindus, custom prevailed of very early betrothal, even at 3 years age, keeping the betrothed in the parents' houses till about 6 when they were put together but the marriage was not consummated till the girl began to menstrurate. The worst havoc that this system played was due to our views on child widows who were either put to the funeral pyre or made playmates by other male members of the family, if not left to fend for themselves. Stigma still remains attached to child widowhood but has enough been done to remove this curse ?

Since we have talked about population explosion, a word about female infanticide, on which there is so much of furore these days. The necessity to adopt all means to have proper birth control has been accepted by all right thinking persons. There can be no objection as such to amniocentesis, the medical test for sex determination in embryo. One is outraged, however, with its resultant effect on the female foetus which is singled out for destruction. Sometimes, some actions which are evil in intent inadvertently lead to betterment of those who righteously feel hurt. Let us take a look back at the beginning of this century and even earlier when due to prolonged wars, the female population in our country in some regions was more vis-a-vis the male population. The result was that parents in their anxiety to see their daughters settled, searched for a partner as early as possible and this led to child marriage, child widows, child prostitution, dowry and polygamy. When the reformists cried out for widow remarriages even such enlightened spirits like Mrs. Annie Besant withheld their support for the noble cause because one widow's remarriage deprived another young girl of her companion. If the number of females is reduced, it will in the long term restrict the brith rate and women's own status may be enhaned due to the restricted application of Malthusianism as the supply and demand equation is bound to have its effect. Postponement of the age of marriage accompanied by strict sexual continence as advocated by the Reverend Malthus, as far back as in 1798, has hardly had any effect anywhere. The Western youth are now going in for early marriages and we are trying to forget sexual restraint. We should therefore, not give undue priorities to our perspective. Why should we weep for one who has not yet seen the light of the day and who has nothing but despair to greet her on arrival? How can we expect the same dreadful parents, who are willing to get their child aborted if, and only if, she is a female, to rear up the young damsel with any care so that she in her time may get all the honour that is due to her?

In this context, let us not ignore the problem of spinsters. If the Western female looked for security, her male counterpart also laid greater emphasis on beauty which is always at a premium. The result is, as brought out by the great Annie Besant, "In the West, there is a large class of unmarried women shut out from all the joys of wifehood and motherhood, and often compelled to earn a precarious living by drudgery and prolonged toil. So numerous are these that the education of women has been revolutionised in order to enable them to compete with men in trades and professions..." [9] The emphasis therefore should be on such measures as would enable our widows, divorcees or spinsters to stand on their own rather than let their numbers, as well as ordeals soar to unmanageable limits. These ladies in their turn should also remember one of the most inspiring verses of Manu which states, "One should not allow one's spirit to be frustrated by earlier failures; one should not disregard oneself; till death one should strive for prosperity and should never consider it difficult of attainment."[10] V. Ragahavan brings out, "It is perhaps this aspect that enthused Nietzche to exclaim about *Manu Smriti* that it has an affirmation of life, a triumphing, agreeable sensation in life, and that to draw up a lawbook such as Manu means to permit oneself to get the upper hand, to beome perfect, to be ambitious of the highest art of living'. " [11] There is nothing that should prevent our single women taking an inspiration from Manu's pronouncement and it is for them to stand up and wipe out the cobwebs of social stigma. A

[9] *The Central Hindu College Magazine*, 1903.

[10] Manu IV.137.

[11] V. Raghavan, *The Cultural Heritage of India*, op.cit., vol. ii, p. 344

change in our outlook is also required. Single independent women, beyond an age, are looked down upon in our society as easily accessible. We must face the reality that the age of one-sided morality is gone past, and these women have a right to live as they want to. However, for their own future happiness, those who have lived an unhappy sexual life should also have the foresight to inform their prospective bridegrooms not to expect a chaste virgin. Why should anyone, male or female, be overtaken or made to suffer by the later confessions of a Thomas Hardy's innocent *Tess of the D'Urbervilles* (1891)?

Fortunately there are hardly any spinsters in our society as both parents as well as the girl desire a normal married life. However, now that some of us want our younger generation to participate in the extravaganza of sexual utopia, would it not lead to a large number of female free-lancers? What a gift we parents, marooned in our craze for advancement, are bestowing on our gifted children! Instead of cautioning them to keep themselves away from the doors of living hell or pull them out of it, we are pushing them to get entangled in the swamp of free sex leaving them with little choice between the devil and the deep blue sea.

19

MOTHER INDIA BECOMES MOTHER-IN-LAW

I have not picked up some malpractices outside India as a gutter inspector, a Katherine Mayo, of 'Mother Europe'. Nor am I 'adopting a holier than thou' stance. Many times one shivers when one comes to know how our elders auctioned our females' chastity. We have had and still have our *devadasis* (female slaves of gods). There were nearly 1,50,000 *devadasis* in 1947. The then Minister of State for Women, Mrs. Margaret Alva, informed Parliament on 18 November, 1987 that this number had since been mounting. These musical organs dancing to glory allow themselves to be tuned up by the priests and then pass the rest of their lives in pecuniary starvation. How class superiority could give open leverage to the Namboodiris, descendants of the great Adishankara, who till very lately could call in any woman in their parlour is symbolic of our passivity. Earlier, what happened in the temples at Benaras, forcing women all adorned to be sliced up by *Kashi karaut* down below in the shaft, showed up the basest instincts that greed for money could bring out in a man who had assumed the authority of celestial power. Indians can no doubt reach any height up to Kailash and Mansarovar but then they can also go so low that a thousand Al Capones would shudder to make the attempt. Let us take two instances which have brought us so down that no Hindu in ages to come would be able to justify his existence and yet some of us are inclined to treat these matters lightly as stale subjects.

Dowry has been a custom since time immemorial, but its fury has now assumed astronomical proportions. Other societies also had this system. It was only with the acquisition of Bombay (1661), received as part of dowry of Catherine of Braganza, daughter of the King of Portugal, to her husband Charles II of England, that the British secured a good base for operations in India. Today, there is no custom, no self-inflicted wound anywhere, that brings upon us even an iota of the shame which this curse, in its present manifestation, has brought on Indian society. We blame the father-in-law, mother-in-law and the husband for the dowry deaths. The greatest blame is on the father himself. First of all, some fathers

(Photo Courtesy: Mr. A. Pasricha)

The trio sisters, Radhika, Shobana and Gayatri. Encouraged by their parents, the group succeeds in its effort to master the carved elegance of Bharatnatyam.

'Listen to the exhortation of the dawn!
Look to this day!
For it is life, the very life of life (verities)
In its brief course lie all the truths and realities of your existence;

the joy of growth, (bliss)
the glory of action,
the splendour of beauty.

For yesterday is but a dream,
and every tomorrow is only a vision;
But today well-lived makes every yesterday a dream of happiness,
and tomorrow a vision of hope.
Look well therefore to this day !
Such is the salutation of the dawn.'

A Sanskrit Prayer

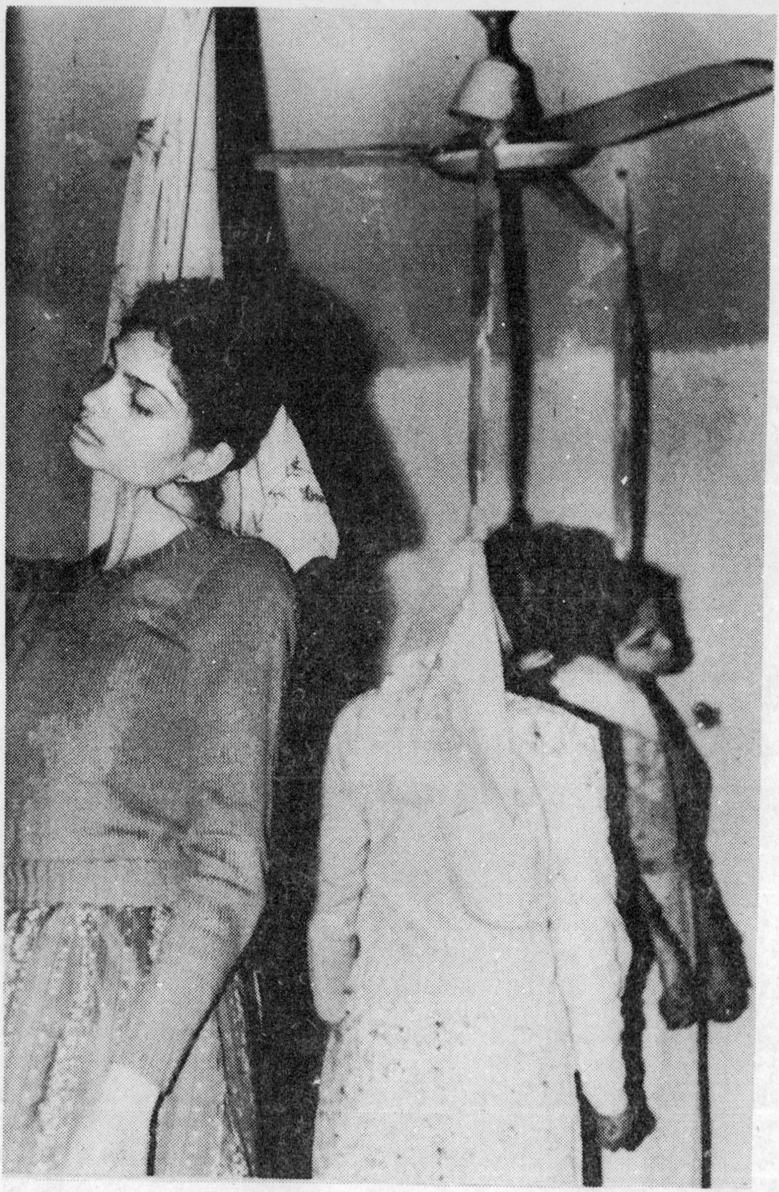

(Photo Courtesy U.N.I.)

Shan't we hang our head in shame? High dowry demands and frequent parading before prospective husbands and in-laws forced these sistrs aged 18, 20 and 22 to commit suicide in the Collie Bazar area of Kanpur in Feb, 88. Where else, we may ask, such a ghastly event occurs in the whole world? Instead of seeking a chance to play a spiritual lead in international affairs, why do we not settle our own horse in order?

"May my eyes never turn away from the world because they are afraid—
and may they never shut on the troubles and despair of human beings.
Grant that my eyes may be startling because they are an encounter with God."

Michel Quoist

some fathers who cannot fulfil the dowry demanded, promise to make it up after marriage, knowing fully well they cannot, in order to get the girl settled in a house beyond reach just to enhance their prestige. Despite knowing later that the girl who is given insufficient dowry is being tortured, she is discouraged from leaving her tyrannical husband. A recent study [1] reveals that 70 per cent of the parents forced their daughters to go back even when they were apprised of perpetual harassment. Out of those who did go back, 77 per cent got deserted and 11.5 per cent got murdered. In most cases, the parents were more willing to put thousands of rupees into the hands of a man who tortured their daughter rather than spend a fraction of the dowry to enable the girl to live independently. We know that in most cases when the demands are met, fresh demands follow. The girl herself, in the majority of cases, even when educated, lacks the courage to stand on her feet. In some extreme cases an unmarried girl who finds her father cannot meet the dowry demand identifies herself as the cause of his suffering and prefers to commit suicide to see the end of his ordeal.

Greed of the in-laws no doubt comes into play and victimisation, even burning to death, follows. People who take pride in deeds of *johar* now let their own greed manipulate immolation as the girl fails to react. Only in a few cases does the girl leave the husband on her own. The result is the typical case where, as reported by the neighbours, the girl was tied with a rope, thrown in the court-yard and beaten till she bled and then set on fire. Her screams were heard by all the neighbours but they were afraid of the hassles that would ensue if they intervened. Such cases get registred, with our most decrepit police, as "accidental burn while cooking" or of suicide. Dowry harassment exists in all religious groups and castes in India. In one study, of 150 victims, 68 per cent were Hindus, 17 per cent were Muslims and 15 per cent Sikhs. (Rajputs 23.5 per cent, Brahmins 18.7 per cent, Khatris 17.6 per cent Scheduled Castes 5.9% of total).[2]

---

[1] *The Times of India*, 16 August, 1987.
[2] *The Times of India*, 16 August, 1987.

The then Minister of State for Home, Mr. P. Chindambaram, told the *Lok Sabha* on 18 November, 1987 that the number of bride burning cases in the capital registered during six months that year had gone up to 239 from 233 during the corresponding period in the previous year. We know that only a fraction of the cases get registered. Did any of the honourable MPs ask the Minister in how many cases so far since Independence had any in-law or husband been hanged or even found guilty of such crime against humanity? Any negro in the strangles of Klu Klux Klan would prefer to be lynched straight rather than undergo such prolonged and unbearable torture leading to incineration. And we, the only propagators of peace, non-vilolence and vegetarianism in this universe, show such apathy to such cannibalistic heinous acts!

The in-laws may be accused of loving easy money. Excess of it may not lead to their happiness but lack of it certainly leads to unhappiness because they feel that they are being deprived of what the genitals of their male child conferred upon them as a right. The shameless excuse offered is that they have to fulfil their obligations towards their female children whom God has cursed them with. But the worst is the scorpion of a husband who would like his wife to come all embellished in order that he may come into instant money. The Hindu boy's position is much freer today; he can divorce and find another E1 Dorado.Why then has he to live the rest of his life as a murderer without remorse? The reason, perhaps, is that this man does not wish to be exposed as a dowry-seeker and as an innocent young widower wants to earn much more in the next round.

Since this evil of dowry cannot be wiped out we must find ways to contain it. We must deny the right of father to deprive his daughter of her share as given to a son unless he takes permission from the court on grounds of disobedience or misconduct or he otherwise compensates her adequately. The father should also muster the courage to say 'no' to any proposal where any demands are put however obliquely. However, if ones does reach a settlement, dowry and/or *stridhan* should be allowed to be given openly under registration without any gift tax and the girl should have the absolute right to get it back whenever she chooses to leave her husband. After marriage, the moment any hints are thrown to the girl to get more money, she should be trained to have the courage to return to her father's house. Parents of the girl should then be obliged to keep their daughter with them as we know that the initial taunts for more money lead to harassment and then to homicide. Instant divorce should be granted in such cases so that the girl may be remarried or encouraged to settle herself in a suitable vocation.

In the recent past they showed on TV a group of male students from Haryana giving their views on dowry. It was disgusting to hear that some of them justified dowry as their right. Should not the same TV have, as a corollary, also interviewed educated girls asking their reactions to dowry intimidation? One solitary case of a woman burnt with whisky poured over her when shown on TV did shake up the ethos of the people. Would it not be better if cases where the girl, to avoid torture, has herself moved away from the in-laws, either back to her father's house or taken up an independent job, are also shown regularly? And if the TV is to do social service, why does it not announce refuge to those helpless brides who are thrown back to the in-laws' den by their parents and who do not know where to go, with no straw in sight to catch hold of, waiting silently for the day when the cooker in the kitchen would be made to burst? One can have full hope, that unless it appears to be a well-planned hoax, which can be seen through in the interviews of parents, the in-laws and the husband, enough funds can be raised by the TV overnight to help the girl find a new lease of life.

And now about *sati*, the most unspeakable ordeal any single helpless woman is made to undergo anywhere today, that is, her being burnt alive on her husband's pyre. The first woman known to history who committed this suicide was Sulochana, wife of Meghanada, son of Ravana, the demon against whom Lord Rama fought in the*treta* age. Had this event ever been prevalent at that time in our society, would not any one of the three queens of Dusratha, father of Lord Rama, not committed *sati*? The first woman known in India who went through this act is Madri, the second wife of Pandu, of a later period the *dwapar*. Could her act not have been motivated by a guilt complex as she was the cause of Pandu's untimely death by letting him be seduced by her, knowing that it would be fatal? And this, when to get a progeny she had the acquiesence of Pandu to get her twin-sons from the physician of the gods? Later, in the middle-ages, the invasions did give a sanctity to the ordeal. On Maharaja Krishnaya Deva, who reigned (1509-29) over the mighty empire of Vijaynagar, "the last of the most splendid of the Hindu empires of southern India", then comprisingm the present states of Tamil Nadu, Karnataka and Kerala, "one traveller tells us that the King had 12,000 wives, of whom, 2000 or 3000 had to burn themselves when he died". [3] What an animal sacrifice and some of us worship this herd as *sati-matas*! What a mockery of companionship on which Rudyard Kipling in his own way jeered when he wrote as if describing a *Charge of the Light Brigade*:

> "The Boondi Queen beneath us cried:
> See, now, that we die as our mothers died
> In the bridal-bed by our master's side
> Out women! – to the fire!" [4]

Some of our acute maniacs and murderers, claiming to re-enact a hoary past, are basically imbibed with greed in order to prevent the share of her dead husband devolving on a young widow. They employ pressure and force to make her perpetually available to her dead husband in heaven or hell wherever he may be. It is her fault that he died and she must pay the price for it even if she was never touched by him. An odd Justice V.R. Krishna Iyer may react against it. But such condemnation gets drowned by the passage of time as was Raja Ram Mohan Roy's and Lord Bentincks' whose joint efforts brought the abolition of *Sati* in 1829. One can do no better than to quote important extracs from the learned Justice's

---

3 Rawlinson, op.cit., pp.157, 162.

4 *The Last Suttee*, *The Works of Kipling*, Black's Readers Service Co., New York, p.56.

opinion.

"*Sati* is a criminal pehnomenon which I believe offends the conscience of humanity. It is murder most foul of Indian women by cultural coercion and the ghastly sanction of incineration. The Deorala episode (1987)... shows how backwardness and primitivism have been preserved in our rural vastness through deadly misinterpretation of scriptures and lethal masculine social pressure... I need only quote Mahatma Gandhi : 'All humanity is one undivided and indivisible family and each one of us is responsible for the misdeeds of all others. I cannot detach myself from the widkedest soul'. Society prepares the crime; the criminal commits it... Is it not a blot on our moral authority internationally that 28 *sati* crimes have been committed since Independence? "5

If humanity is indivisible, we should be made answerable by some International Court of Justice for such crimes which are worse than what any Botha can think of. We owe it to our manhood and our future generations, not to talk of poor women, that *sati*, this *johar* in reverse, and its glorification, is put an immediate halt to. This hideous activity lay dormant so long as Gandhiji was alive.[5] . If the King of Belgium can now be expected to save our wild life, if the great Brigitte Bardot can forsake her eternal charm to look after the animal kingdom, cannot there be some Florence Nightingale, a Joan of Arc or a Sarojini Naidu anywhere in this universe to stand up for the guiltless Indian womanhood being strangulated under the emasculated Indian male? Even Mrs. Indira Gandhi, the *Durga Mata*, failed to stem the rot when she was fully in the saddle. If this act is voluntary on the part of a woman, then it is nothing but psychological enslavement to the condemnable Necrophilia (a morbid love or horror for the dead), and this maniacal manifestation of suicide must be rooted out and all accomplices hanged by the nearest pole. But we blind ourselves to reality when when we are told that there is no coercion involved. Imagine a woman being drugged into semi-consciousness with opium, forcibly escorted by men with open swords in their hands

---

5 *The Hindustan Times*, 4 October, 1987.

to the pyre, her half burnt body being repeatedly thrust back on it even as she lets out blood-curdling cries for mercy which get drowned in the chants of '*Sati mata ki jai*' all being enacted under the garb of religion, faith and tradtion.

As for support accorded to this infamous practice by an act of priestly forgery, Mr. S Natrajan, the founder of that influential journal, *Indian Social Reformer*, says: "Later Orientalists like Wilson and Max Müller were to maintain that the one line in the *Rig Veda* which was held to enjoin *sati*, was a deliberate distortion. 'Perhaps the most flagrant instance of what can be done by an unscrupulous priesthood', wrote Max Müller."[6]

Meanwhile, Parliament has passed the Sati Prevention Bill. Will it be implemented effectively? Let us keep our fingers crossed.

---

6 *A Century of Social Reform in India*, Asia Pubishing House, Bombay, 1959, p.34.

20

ALL THAT GLITTERS IN THE WEST OF INDIA IS NOT GOLD

The attempt to lift our people, from orthodoxy and suppression takes my mind back to what Mr. Hirschfeld said in his inaugural address to the First Congress of the World League for Sexual Reforms on a Scientific Basis in Berlin in 1921:

"The sexual needs of the majority of human beings have just as imperative a demand for occasional fulfilment as the need for food and sleep. The best way of living is to avoid either starvatio.. or surfeit and keep the via media between a necessary minimum of activity and experience and a maximum which shall not prove intolerable to the powers and the balance of personality... In the history of human love, three stages may be differentiated. In the earliest of these, sexuality was mainly a reflex mechanism, as amongst lower creatures. There followed a second stage in which we now are (1921). In this phase inhibitive mechanism became paramount. Humanity has constructed codes of different kinds which find expression in contemporary customs and morals. Thus in the second phase we find the most fantastic ethical and practical extremes. Compulsory virginity and compulsory prostitution for instance and even extravagant opposites. But for the last few decades there has been a new light on humanity's horizon which slowly grows. The third stage in the history of human love must establish harmony between inhibitions and reflexes. It must avoid indiscriminate licence and indiscriminate abstinence, the abstinence which Edward Carpenter so well called 'the renunciation of this world for its shadow". [1]

There is a thin dividing line between the first and the third stages of this mathematics of sex wherein in the new stage a little harmony was advocated to be established between inhibitions and reflexes. Little, perhaps, it was visualised that a fourth stage would

---

[1] *Woman*, op.cit., vol. i, p. 121.

soon come up allowing society to be all permissive and hardly any difference would be left between "loving" and "making love".

In India there has never been open sexual reflex mechanism except among odd tribes. As in Europe earlier, as illustrated in the compendium *Woman*, with diagrams, we have never had torture chambers, apparatus for masochistic performances and sadistic establishments for satisfaction of sex. We haven't had, excision, the circumcision of girls intended to set bounds to the sexual impulse of the women as among some Arabs.[2] The exclamation 'Oh, son of an uncircumcised woman' is one of the deepest affronts in their huge vocabulary of insults, according to G.A. Wilkan.[3] We will not talk of infabulation done in Africa, the 'sewing up' where excision was so arranged that it allowed only urinary opening simply in order to enforce complete abstinence. Hartmann says, "Slaves too are infabulated thus. These are cruel masters— and some of them are Europeans — who have had this thing done even twice or thrice to the same women who have been their mistresses — and then sold them". [4] We have not had the need of the 'girdle of chastity' with which knightly forefathers in Europe clothed their wives before they themselves rode forth on the Crusades. We have also not had reports like that of Mr. W.T. Stead [5] which caused a sensation with its accounts of the trade in virgins in England, in which he stated that means were employed to simulate virginity in deflowered girls.

Let us further see some of the ugly facets of development. "Throughout the Middle Ages and Renaissance clerical celibacy was a social evil. When it was genuine it impaired the race, sterilised and secluded many excellent elements; when it was not

---

2 *La femme arabe dans la province de Union Med.*, Paris, 1865; *Woman*, op.cit., vol.i, p. 341.

3 *Das Matrianchat bei den alten araben*, Leipzig, 1884; Woman, op.cit., vol.i, p.341.

4 *Woman*, op.cit., vol. i, p. 362.

5 *The Maiden Tribute of Modern Babylon*, London, 1885; *Woman*, op.cit., vol.i., p.359.

genuine, it was a focus of immorality which undermined the reputation of women".[6] The convents for nuns originated almost simultaneously with the monastries for monks. "But the life of pious ecstasy and self-mortification gave place after a few centuries to freer conception of human existence... There exists even at the present time in many places an underground passage connecting famous convents (certainly not without a purpose) with the neighbouring monastry. From the secretary of Pope Urban VI (1378-1389), Theodoricus de Niem, we have a ghastly picture of vile life which the holy virgins led with the monks and with the priests set on authority over them."[7] In sharp contrast is the terrible severity in many of them towards the unfortunate virgins of God who had broken the vow of chastity. The more severe penances, fasting and whipping awaited them and in many cases they expiated their sin with death, which was brought about usually be their being buried or walled up alive."[8]

One wonders as to why such a wrath was put on the innocent daughters of the Virgin when the whole atmosphere was vitiated as we see in Europe in the 15th Century. "The Public bath houses of the town, also, where men and women, maidens and youth, monks and nuns bathe together quite naked could certainly not promote chastity".[9] Being undressed or all dressed up has never been much of a barrier. A study of Alexander Pope's (1688-1744), *Rape of the Lock* hints at the upheavel in the elite caused by sweet melodies in the masquerades resulting in orgy in mass in the ball room itself where a lord in his own rapture did not know with whom his daughter was on the same floor. These frivolities also pale into insignificance when we see the facileness prevailing in one of the

---

[6] *Woman*, op.cit., vol.i, p.537. See for satire Henry C. Lea's, *History of Sacerdotal Celibacy in the Christian Church*, London, 1907, IIIrd Edition.

[7] *Hist. Sui Temporis Libri IIII, Argentorat*, 1609; *Woman*, op.cit., vol. ii, p.271.

[8] *Woman*, op.cit., vol.ii, p.276.

[9] J. Scherr, *Deustche Kultre Und Sittergeschichte*, Leipzig, 1858; *Woman*, op.cit., vol.ii, p.13.

most polished nations of Europe in the times of Emperor Charles V: "On his state entries the daughters of nobles considered it an honour to parade before him stark naked, and it is well known that fathers willingly surrendered their daughters to the Emperor as concubines". [10]

Animals, we are told, are all regulated by nature. But how well can the animals be trained to brighten one's lives? Nehru wondered, in another context, "What these animals and birds think of man and how they would describe him if they had the capacity to do so". [11] Plutarch tells us that from the earliest times women abandoned themselves to the caprice of the sacred goats in Mendes.[12] Some attribute the advent of VD to the adventures of the lone shepherd in the wild deserts with the she goat. Man is a social animal. Forced loneliness, unless wedded to a higher ideal, knows no other end except self-destruction.

Let us see how a past master offers some sympathy for the ordeals gone through in search of harmony. "Shepherds were a class apart... From infancy they followed their calling, which took them in all seasons and weathers, day and night, into the hills and condemned them to loneliness and brute company. With manhood they became sullen, while a few turned dangerously savage, more animal than man, haunting the flocks, and finding the satisfaction of their adult appetites in them, to the exclusion of more licit affections."[13]

Later, it is the dog which takes the pride of place. "Sometimes charming women in the highest circles of the most cultivated society of Europe adore their lap dogs for reasons which they would not confess to a living soul except perhaps to their confessor... Archbishop Claret directed confessors to ask their

---

[10] *Munster, Sebastian, Cosmographie Oder Beschrubung aller Länder*, Basel, 1548; *Woman*, op.cit., vol. ii, p. 15.

[11] E. P. Gee, The Wildlife of India, London, 1964, p.5.

[12] *Opera Parisiis*, 1841-1855, *Woman*, op.cit., vol.ii, p.76.

[13] T.E. Lawrence of Arabia, op.cit., p.206.

female penitents on these delicate matters." [14]

We no doubt see in stone a lion mating with a damsel at Khajuraho. Perhaps the sole original intention was an imaginative display of a religious conception, inspired by the gods of procreation requiring a man to be as powerful as a lion rather than highlight a woman's competence or a prevalent custom. We also see depicted in just a few temples, "Couples in coitus, in positions hardly conceivable to the boldest imagination that give evidence of a fairly high degree of craftsmanship on the part of the sculptor."[15] May be works of imagination, but nobody can deny that these are faultily faultless pieces of art depicting mind and body, both of man and woman, each giving off the best of their inner self to attain a perfect unison of full and equal involvement.

In these temples there is never any evidence of homosexuality or 'Sapphic love' which is wide-spread outside. Lately, I found myself unknowingly entering a lesbian night club in Athens, the second intellectual capital of Europe, the other no doubt being Paris. What an unwanted guest I was! Just as well we didn't have any poetess like Sappho, the native of Lesbos, (Greece, c.600 B.C.) whose lyrics sowed the seeds of unnatural passion between women so deep that the cult of Sapphism lives to see light till today in the delusion of gender. Perhaps these adherents have joined up in revolt against an earlier Western thought : "Woman", Virchow is reported to have said, "is a pair of ovaries with a human being attached, whereas man is a human being furnished with a pair of testes."[16] The entire concept of love thus got warped, the woman becoming just an object meant to titillate and be tilled by the male.

And for those who may be over-awed by the possibility of being over-laid in an unfortunate encounter, a new courage is being

---

[14] A.M. Claret, *Lave de Oro*, Pablo Rira, 1860. *Aliquando ponens Salivan aut panem in vas et gogens canum ut lambat etc etc*. Woman, op.cit., vol.ii, p.76.

[15] *The Antiquities of Orissa*, Calcutta, 1875.

[16] *Woman*, op.cit., vol. ii, p. 361.

imparted by a stalwart, Germaine Greer, who advises: "Rape is sexual intercourse, i.e. intromission, with a woman who does not give her consent. Women who believe that penetration against their will lays them waste or destroys their bodily integrity are accepting the male exaggeration of the power and importance of a relatively harmless and extremely vulnerable member... Just as virginity is not destroyed when the hymen is perforated (sic), woman's integrity is not destroyed by outrge, unless she identifies herself as the vessel that the man has used. To regard oneself as destructible in this way is to internalise the reification, i.e. the treating of a woman as a thing, that male culture inflicts on women's personhood...

"All men are rapists... It makes no sense to glamourise a tiny proportion of them foolish or feeble or crazy enough to be caught in the act of grand rape by exaggerating the genital compenent of their crime. To do so perpetuates the psychopathy of everyday sex hostility..."[17]

As to the insinuation that every man is a rapist, I leave it to the white man to defend himself. Apparently, there is in big spurt in his activity. some European ladies confide that earlier, when they were young, they could have a quiet stroll in the evenings by the riverside in their town; now they dare not, for fear of being waylaid by maniacs putting women down to earth for trying to achieve economic equality!

Be that as it may, the points brought out above regarding what forms and attitudes sex can take or spark off outside India was to prove that all that glitters in the west of India is not gold. The real West, America, initially inhabited by the European outcastes, has hardly had the time or the patience to go through the three stages of love as in Europe. The Americans seem to have taken all the three stages together in one mighty hop, step and jump to have a head on plunge in sexual abyss. Today, "some 12 million American teenagers are sexually active, some beginning at the age of 13 or

---

17 *The Hindustan Times*, 13 September, 87

younger. Children are fed on the delusion that sex is an immediate and urgent necessity. In America, one half million teenagers contacted gonorrhoea in 1985. Syphilis and genital herps (skin diseases) reached epidemic limits in the '80s. In addition, teenagers have to face the problems of miscarriages, still brith and congenitally deformed children. Cases of blindness, deafness and other diseases have also been caused by sexually transmissable diseases, not to mention depression, anxiety and acute feeling of loneliness. In a letter to the Times, Mr. Howard Marratt, Vice Chairman of the National Religious Education Council, blames the current violence and sexual promiscuity on a lack of religious and moral education."[18]

Let us, however, not get carried away by the false notion that sex has ruined the American life. If that was so, America woud not have become the number one Super Power in a short span of few centuries. Sex certainly has made a major dent in the fabric of American communal life, but it has not been so domineering or damaging as to lessen the zeal to scale new heights. Downgradation of sex, making it a follow up course, as a dessert after dinner or a corollary to a 'date' with any stranger, may have taken out the penchant for love and human bondage but not for nothing can the Americans boast of the maximum number of Nobel laureates.Their quest for retaining their supremacy and develop further has been unparalleled since their inception. If the initial settlers needed manpower, Africa was made the sellers' market for slaves. The negress was always available as an outlet but if the black male, who found himslef sought after by the white woman, succumbed to pressure or temptation thrown at him, there was nothing except lynching as his reward. Till today, a person with even 1/16th of the black blood is not legally acceptable to the *nouveau riche* as a legitimate companion. Later, as more manpower was needed the door was kept wide open for any white man. Western Europe thus got rid of its poor and America till now remains a land of opportunity for them. That in the process the low-placed white seekers of haven have to give up their language,

---

[18] T. Karanjia, *Eve's Weekly*, 18-24 July, 87.

culture and way of life in a tribute to Uncle Sam. A redeeming feature is that some semblance of religion is still left in the sense that few call themselves atheists openly. One cannot also restrain from paying tribute to the American women who by dauntless courage, after a long struggle, have achieved near equal status with men in their performance. Piloting USAF combat planes, they are not content to be left *hors de combat.*

What about the other Supper Power, founded on the notion of the infallible Karl Marx that "religion is the opiate of the masses"? Let us have a distant look.

21

COMMUNISTIC CONCUBINAGE

Lenin's advocacy of the abolition of the abominable bourgeois institution called marriage may have failed due to inherent self-contradictions in the Soviet system based on the high-flown principle, 'To each according to his needs'. The married Soviet couple thus got entitled to better accommodation, say in some cases two roomed, rather than each single person having a corner in small room, Napolean had advised his troops to 'march separately and strike together.' In their march forward to live better, the Soviet youth readapted the reactionary system of marriage but kept the red flag flying by concurrently regaling in adultery separately in their different rooms while living together under the same roof as wedded couple. Bonds of marriage imposed no bar to the proliferation of a classless society which had got out of the theological opium-den to look for mid-night oil in domestic taverns. And yet one hears echoes of male chauvinism. What a fine social stability, product of Marx and Engels and all the Angels put together!

We of course find it simpler to censure anything that we consider wrong when we see it in the non-communist white world. More often than not the condemnation sprouts up within their own millieu of which we may or may not be even aware. What, in any case, is admirable is that everything is open in a free society which has the option to accept or reject any idea or practice. From the closed Communist utopia only self-opinionated praise comes out. We have to learn from the observations made by independent commuters about what is happening behind the Iron Curtain.

Drinking may not be the effect but it certainly is the cause or the mother or prostitution, illicit affairs and open sex. The two evils are inseparable. No people in this world are reported to be hitting the bottle so hard as the progenies of the revolutionised proletariat who, in their struggle to throw away all shackles, have rejected out of hand any semblance of morality. Their own hierarchy, is now forced to admit that it is treating the problem of alcoholism as a national quandary. On the other hand, what one hears of the effect of sexual revolution in the Eastern utopia hardly seems to have caused any widespread concern, for apparently there is hardly anything left of the moral codes to dilate upon.

Whether lack of religious and moral education could be the cause for many a woman parading their ware in the Red Square for roubles or dollars is a subject in the domain of the Supreme Soviet Politburo. What about the less fortunate satellite states of Eastern Europe? Some impartial visitors inform that if an explorer has the wherewithal of Scotch and dollars, he could be a sought after guest in young girls' homes so that international harmony may prevail. Some of the lost souls of Eastern Europe, yearning for the basic amenities of life, have also been made to discard all that can bring domestic happiness. Earlier, in their crusade for progress they were made to throw away religion lock, stock and barrel. Today, they rise in revolt to get it back in its most catholic form and a Pole, the well-timed Pope [1] has to be allowed in to personally pacify the mortified souls in a part of the Empire. What a self-inflicted wound; what a momentary remedy! We now learn that Mr. Bush[2] has also gone to the bush to set bushes about without of course allowing himself to be bushed.

Revolt against exploitation does force one to take to extreme measures. This does not necessarily mean that one should dismantle the basic foundations on which mankind has survived and which have nurtured its evolution for so long. By all means weed out the decomposed and decaying elements but in the process one should not, like the proverbial monkey, chop off the very branch on whose wrong end one is sitting: for, the fall is bound to be fatal. Perhaps some *perestroika* (restructuring) or some *glasnot* (openness) may some day restore some belief in the indispensable humanistic values which were pushed down the Volga decades ago. The new policy is already showing some effect. Now

---

[1] Pope John-Paul II.

[2] Mr. George Bush, President of USA, 1989

someone can at least muster the courage to divulge some facts without dreading the midnight knock and without being pulled out from his home as used to happen during the Stalinistic *Darkness at Noon.*

Now one does get a glimpse of actual social life in the Soviet Union. According to a recent Moscow report, a public survey conducted by the Soviet Centre for Public Opinion notes that, "divorce is very common in the Soviet Union today and the country is close on the heels of the US in the number of cases... Sociologists are raising some uncomfortable questions regarding the changing values of family life. One specialist, Vitaly Tretyakov, asks whether people were prepared for consequences of pre-marital sex, especially among young people. Even school students lead the world in abortions and babies abandoned in maternity homes. He urges a new social policy in conclusion".[3]

How much will a new social policy help? At present, Soviet women have 10 times more abortions than in other developed countries. With 5.5 million children born in the USSR every year, there are seven million abortions. "Financial losses are the easiest to compute", muses Baranov. (Deputy Minister of Health, Dr. Alexander Baranov). "Forty percent of beds in the gynaecology wards are occupied by women undergoing that operation. It is done free of charge in hospitals and women are given three-day paid sick-leaves. The economists say abortions cost a billion roubles a year. Who can compute the damage to health? After an abortion, many women have miscarriages or premature births, which often end in death. Or if it is the first pregnancy, the woman may be left sterile. Why do you think we have 15 million childless families ? "[4]

On the crucial first pregnancies, we have another report:

"Ninety percent of all first pregnancies in the Soviet Union end

---

[3] *The Times of India*, 29 Aug.88

[4] *Physician Heal Thyself*, *Hamari Goshthi*, Indo-Soviet Women's Magazine, No.4, New Delhi, 1988.

in abortion and hundreds of women die each year as a result of the operation, the weekly *Moscow News* reported on Thursday, Reuter reports. The article by Yekaterina Nikolayeva, who recently had an abortion, said women were treated as though they were on an assembly line, so routine has the operation become in the Soviet capital. Official figures show there are eight million abortions in a year in the Soviet Union, probably the highest in the world. 'Every year between 600 to 700 women die as the result of an abortion in the Russian federation alone' , Nikolayeva wrote." [5] Reasons for the widespread practice of abortion in the case of first pregnancies have not been clearly given. Drive for birth control cannot be the sole motivating factor for surely one can achieve it by aborting subsequent efforts. What one may infer is that either a large percentage of the babies aborted are illegitimate or the Soviet youth wish to continue with uninterrupted sex without being burdened with the responsibility to rear up the young ones. The excuse offered by some Russians in personal talks of financial constraint in maintaining the child is hardly tenable.

Further South, China is also reported to be going through a fall out in the domestic field.Current news from the 'Good Earth', one-time land of pig-tails, brings out the breaking up caused by the 'Cultural Revolution'. A Beijing report says: "The divorce rate among young married couples in China's big cities is skyrocketing, with many of them married for only one or two years, the *China Daily* reported on Wednesday, says *Xinhua*. The paper says by the time 100 urban couples go to a studio to have their wedding photographs taken, 30 couples in the same city go to the court or civil affairs department to register for divorce. Wang Deyi, chief of the marriage administration department, is quoted as saying that 5,00,000 couples got divorced in 1987. Civil affairs departments handled 2,30,000 of the cases and the remainder were handled by the courts".[6]

One of course does not know whether in the Communist world

---

[5] *The Times of India*, 21st January, 1989.

[6] *The Times of India*, 30 March, 1989

they have heard the word 'Self-restraint'. But it is heartening to hear the views of Lidia Grigorieva, Russian poetess and literary critic, and a defender of women's emancipation. On "Women's Mission" she says:

"I remember how bitterly I cried in a blossoming garden when I finished Leo Tolstoy's novel *War and Peace*. I was seventeen then and felt disappointed, cheated and humiliated by the end of that great book. Is it going to be my lot? Swaddling-clothes, spots on them, and primitive, yes, primitive love for the babies? Never. I am superior to all that and will never be a Natasha Rostova. The heroine of *War and Peace* was so extraordinary and romantic and ingenuous at the beginning, and what has become of her! I won't play the second fiddle. After all I have equal rights with men. The right sort of woman will never accept such a lot. She will wish to be something more than an ideal wife and mother... Now twenty years later I look at the young anti-woman I was with a smile of understanding and condescension. The fact that emancipation is being overstretched worries me now. Women should not abide by the rules of the man's world. Women are fragile and weaker than men. For all their aspirations for absolute equality, they must leave to the man what is his. An age of manly women and womanly men must never come. Step every our threshold, I will tell my son, but look back at your home, your ancestors and mother. I rejected this though when I was young, then lost it in the rapid succession of events and only regained it through much soul searching. The simpler and weightier a thought is, the greater the zeal with which it is rejected by youth and regained by maturity. "[7]

Such soul-searching is perhaps the only panacea of many social ills in the advanced world. Let us hope there are more such searches done in both the capitalist and Communist worlds in this field and the revelations may help us retain our heritage.

Before we close this chapter, we may as well remember that despite all advancement, neither the Old nor the New world have

---

[7] *Hamari Goshthi*, op.cit.

shed their prejudice against the fair sex. There is still a heavy hangover of the old-fashioned traditional attitude towards women and their rights. Even an apparently civilised country like Switzerland did not give its women voting rights until 1971. What is most surprising is that the Soviet Union, the 'examplary' Socialist society, has only recently appointed one woman to its Central Committee which amounts to one out of several hundred men. There are no women ministers and none in the Politburo of the Communist Party of the Soviet Union. In Hungary, Mrs. Duschek, President of the National Council of Women, admitted that in spite of a law passed in 1945 establishing equality of pay, women still get 30 per cent less than men. In the U.S. about 50 per cent of the women now work, but they are still lagging behind in terms of equal pay.

Let the gorgeous West and Super Powers design their own pattern. Why should we allow it to be the template which should mould and freeze our way of life? We have enough problems on our own hands which should be resolved before we submerge ourselves in sexual euphoria.

22

A CRY FROM A DISTANT LAND—BULGARIA

We are not the only people who have been through the pangs of slavery. One can safely say that there are no people on any side of this earth who have not been subjugated or subjected to defeat at one time or the other. Yet only those who are not ashamed to admit what they went through, see the why of it, and are not hesitant to take corrective measures can hold on to their own. On the other hand, people who forget, ignore or sidetrack history are condemned to rerun through slavery which always brings untold sufferings on women enslaved. As a first step one has to go through historical facts. The pity is that more often than not it is the historians themselves who falsify history to such as extent that the German philosopher, Schaupenhauer, was provoked to jibe that, "all history books were as infested with lies as a public woman with syphilis! " However, by analysing both sides of a story, as well as by examining the orders given to the rank and file who executed them in the course of their mission , one can draw correct perspective. Here we have time to take up only one such case.

Bulgaria is a small country — small in numerical sense. I have not chosen it because the Bulgarians are now exploring links between ancient Bulgarian and Indian scriptures or because their prominent scholar Kaner devoted his whole life to translating the *Vedas* into Bulgarian or for that matter because of Gurudev Tagore's marvellous description of this land and its people when he visited it in 1926. The reason is that these people went through certain facets of slavery with which we have some commonalty.

The Bulgarians give a vivid account of the ordeals they went through when their small territory of 110,900 square km became a province of the Ottoman Empire founded by Sultan Murad I (1360-1389), their population then being just about 5 million. They bring out their sorrow through a documentary series, *Archives Speak*

Volumes[1] which brings out:

"The conversion of Bulgarians to Islam during the years of Bulgarians' conquest and thereafter, was carried out in various forms... such as direct physical compulsion involving the threat of life, enslavement in its specific varieties and economic compulsion ... the Islamization of the Bulgarian people was precipitated by taking away and enslavement of children, girls and young brides who were sold and sent as sevants in the harems while some of the girls were compelled to marry Moslems... Another equally widespread form of enslavement was the janissary system."[2]

Janissaries were members of the regular infantry in the Ottoman empire. "The Janissary Corps was set up in 1361 and was initially recruited from prisoners of war and boys taken into slavery. Having been forcibly Islamized and having passed a course of military training the janissaries became the main military and internal political force in the empire."[3] The *firman* of the Sultan issued in 1546 reads: "For a long time now there is a law and a tradition to select children (Christians) for the janissary corps.This is now the reason why the present imperial *firman* is published. I order that they be chosen from each village and hamlet..." [4] The execution of the order implied that, "The children from the region subject to levy were selected in front of the Governor's residence and — stripped naked — were examined thoroughly. The next procedure was the circumcision (*sunnet*) which was accompanied by the acceptance of a voluntarily chosen or imposed Moslem name..."[5] By the time of Mahmud II (1809 - 1839), the Janissary Corps numbered 1,40,000. The report laments, "The early

---

[1] Sophia Press Agency, Vols. 1-4, 1984 onwards.

[2] Vol. 3, pp.3-4.

[3] Vol. 4, pp.9.

[4] Written in the last ten days of the month of *Ramadan* 943/May 29 — June 7, 1546. This document is kept at the Deparment of Oriental Studies of the National Library in Cairo under the press mark M-48; vol.2, pp.17-19.

[5] vol. 2, pp. 5,8.

Ottoman chroniclers did not fail to mention that thousands of slaves, mostly lovely girls and boys 'as beautiful as the sun' were taken away. In hundreds of songs the Bulgarian people have poured out their pain for their lost daughters, wives, sisters and mothers. Apart from that these same people were implacable as regards the women's doom: after marrying men of a differet religious creed they were considered dead. The folk songs had it that parents cursed bitterly their daughters whose beauty had attracted the Turks and would rather have them dead".[6]

Forced conversions, whenever imposed anywhere, have always aroused indignation. In 1844, after five centuries of oppression in Bulgaria, reforms had to be announced by the then Sultan guaranteeing freedom of religious denominations.We wonder whether his call for compassion was caused by the same perturbations of the 'still small voice', making one see 'only the divinity' which Aurangzeb noticed much earlier in 1707. Perhaps, decline and fall make one see reason. The Sultan's order directed: "None of the subjects of my great state can be forced to become a Moslem without his own consent. Yet, for some time now there have been instances in some places of my well protected kingdom, where, contrary to the above conditions, some of the subjugated Christians, mostly women, children and minors have been pressed to adopt the Islam rather violently and insistently against their will. Informing about all this the Patriarchates this time beg and insist that these practices should be banned..."[7]

The April 1876 Bulgarian uprising led to the secession of big parts of the Ottoman Empire. Now reports are coming of forcible re-Bulgarianisation carried out from late 1984 onwards. Let us see one case:SHTILYAL ASSENOV YULIANOV/Shaban Hyuseyinov, says "... My name was Shaban; Shaban is an Arabic name. I wanted my restored Bulgarian name to have the gentleness

---

[6] Vol.4, pp.3-8.

[7] Written in the last decade of the month of *Safer*, year 1260/13-21. III.1844. This document is preserved in the Cyril and Methodius National Library, Sofia – Oriental department, Sign. OAK 191/15. Vol. I, pp.31-32.

and sonority of the Bulgarian tongue... Why did I do it? You cannot quench what is not for quenching. The truth about our Bulgarian roots is rising from a long sleep..."

One can always quench one's thrist but can one say that those who are 'rising from a long sleep' and changing their names in Bulgaria are inspired only by longing for ancient heritage? It may be safely deduced that it also involves moving away from Islam. There is no indication whether those who are adopting Bulgarian names are reaffirming their faith in Christ or discarding religion in toto.

On this point, one cannot help quoting an observation made by Mr. Konstantin Grigorov (b.1921), a professional diplomat who was Bulgarian Ambassador to China (1973-77) and USA (1977-80): "Bulgarian Moslems are part of the Bulgarian nation. They have all rights and liberties that the Constitution and laws of Bulgaria grant to Bulgarian citizens... However, circumcision of male children at home is prohibited, as such an operation must be done by specialists in clinics for reasons of hygiene and health as stipulated by the law."[8]

This seemingly forthright assertion, like most diplomatic statements, is not devoid of anomalies. What one would like to know is why the chopping off just 1/8th of an inch, as done by the Jews and the Mohammadans at home for ages, now requires it to be done under strict medical regulations? We know the Christians in revolt against Judaism discarded the practice and the Mohammadems in their turn readopted it. Trademarks have their various manifestations. Who knows whether the present laws stipulate that the option can be exercised only after a child is grown up and after enough education has been given to him to know what is good for him? We shall not talk of brainwashing. It remains debatable, however, whether those who shed a religion they were forced to accept should also, when they reassert themselves, throw

---

[8] Rights for All, Co-operation for the Good of Everyone, Sophia Press, 1988, p.28.

God out — root and branch.

Religion is not the opiate of people. It represents a very important dimension of life. It shows a light and brings a fulfilment for which there can never be a substitute . To deny human beings the inner satisfaction which sweeps through mind, body and soul by the worship of a divine force is to maim the life of a people. One religion is a good as another in at least one respect that it guides and inspires one to adhere to a particular code of conduct.And without any established principles anyone can be led astray to lewdness and lawlessness. Submission to a higher spirit does help one to keep on a straight path and when one deviates too much the inner conscience revolts.

In out context, Gandhiji's assassination by a Hindu fanatic spelt disaster for our chauvinists. Sometimes later, Mr. Mohammad C. Chagla, who became Chief Justice of India's Supreme Court and our representative at the U.N., calling for unity in the country advised his co-religionists to remember that there was no Muslim in India in whose veins Hindu blood did not flow. This admission has certainly pulled the carpet from under the feet of either of the die-hards.

It is time, therefore, to ponder as to how we shape our future. Instead of living in lost glories of one's co-religionists or ruing over our past mistakes, a positive course of action is required to be adopted.

23

THE RISE AND FALL OF THE BRAHMANICAL ORDER

For us the word Brahmanism is synonymous with Hinduism. For some in the world till today any Indian is a Hindu and Brahmanism is the dominant religion of India, full of outdated orthodox dogmas which loosely govern the backward polytheists. India is still considered by some to be the Indies, scattered islands inhabited by primitive poor tribes with no semblance of any unity, exotic in many ways, who can never get together and should be shown the light as was done in the East Indies or West Indies or Africa. In 1961, the library books of the French Embassy in India had the old stamp put on them, *L'Ambassade de la France Aux Indes* (Embassy of France in the Indies). In 1962, I was working in the United Nationas HQ in the Congo, just then given freedom by the Belgians. I had invited some friends including an American negro, a senior UN official. The latter flabbergasted me, in my own apartment, when he openly doubted as to how we Indians, an undeveloped people, without any technical background, who did not produce enough to eat and whose every third *chapati* (bread) was made out of the US gifted PL 480 wheat, could think of making any ingress in the scientific or atomic fields. I recalled what the Chairman of our Atomic Energy Commission, Dr. Homi Jehangir Bhabha, a Parsee, had said. Asked, while in the USA, whether India had the thinking power capable to make the bomb, he smilingly replied that the Indians could do so if they wanted to and reminded his audience that the Brahmins had been meditating up in the Himalayas for ages, not for nothing but to sharpen their brains primarily to educate their people.

It may be considered out of context to probe into the vast field of power wielded by Brahmins in a work concerning women. But how can we separate the master from the pupil? Let us therefore see some aspects which had a bearing on the fair sex and our social life on which the *gurus* laid emphais from time to time.

In ancient India, military, political and financial powers were under the guidance of spiritual authority. The Brahmin was expected to do nothing for his own enjoyment. As social responsibility and the desire for personal enjoyment cannot go together, the relation between them being of inverse proportion, those who occupied the highest rank in social hierarchy led a life of simplicity, renunciation and self-denial. In time, our society was divided into four mutable clsses based on professional pursuits of intellect, arms, commerce or menial labour.[1] The basic foundations of Brahmanism and Indian way of life were laid by Manu in *Manu Dharma-Sastra* in the Epic age and expounded by Valmiki and Vyas in the two great Epics of the *Ramayana* and the *Mahabharata,* which have throughout been the foundations of Hindu ethics and beliefs. As we have seen, both the seers, Valmiki and Vyas, belonged to the fourth class, the lowest in their times. It must be said to the credit of the Brahmins that in their quest for intellecutal advancement they never ceased to learn from anyone, howsoever lowly placed the source.

The Aryans coming from Central Asia, from the pasture - lands between the Oxus and Syr Darya rivers, fanned out not only to India but also westwards. The presence of numerous age-old *Sivalings* in South Russia and Egypt are pointers to this fact. There is hardly any doubt left that the worship of *Sivalings* was originated by the Hindus and *Sivaling* means not only *lingam*, the male organ, but equally well *yoni* , that of the female, both the components held and worshipped together in perpetual harmony, without the *yoni* the *lingam* being rootless. On the far flung ancientness of some other Hindu forms of worship, Tod clarified, "That a system of Hinduism pervaded the whole Babylonian and Assyrian empires, Scripture furnishes abundant proofs, in the mention of the various

[1] How a fifth class, the *achoot*, the untouchable, also came into being later can only be attributed to the growth of urban life and the adoption of the dry system involving carrying the dirt manually which caused the relegation of poor scavengers to this class. Unless the wet system is enforced, no legislation or vote catching speeches are likely to remove this blot which is unparalleled in the whole world. Is it not time that we got rid of this foul system?

types of the sun-god Balnat'h, [2] whose pillar adorned 'every mount' and 'every grove'; and to whose other representative, the brazen calf (*nanda*), the 15th of each month(*amavus*) was especially sacred. It was not confined to these celebrated regions of the East, but was disseminated throughout the earth; becaause from the Aral to the Baltic, colonies were planted from that central region, the cradle of the *Suryas* and the *Indus*, whose branches(*sachae*), the *Yavan*, the *Aswa*, and the *Meda*, were the progenitors of the Ionians, the Assyrians and the Medes; while in latter times, from the same teeming region, the Galati and Getae, the Kelts and Goths, carried modifications of the system to the shores of Armorica and the Baltic, the cliffs of Caledonia, and the remote isles of the German Ocean. The monumental circles sacred to the sun-god Belenus at once existing in that central region [3] , in India [4] , and throughout Europe, is conclusive..." [5] .

Rawlinson says that, "The Aryans entered India in successive waves, not as an invading army but as settlers, bringing with them their wives and children and flocks and herds... As they advanced they encountered stiff opposition from the earlier inhabitants... who were highly civilised and dwelt in walled cities. The Indo-Aryans... called them *Dasyus* or *Dasas* (slaves). But they did not exterminate the *Dasyus*. They intermarried with them and descendants of these marriages adopted many of the customs and even the gods of the older race."[6] The sage Agastya is credited with grammatising the Tamil language. A sobering influence thus

---

2 "The temple of Solomon was to Bal, and all the idolators of that day seem to have held the grosser tenets of Hinduism". Tod, op.cit., vol.i, p.64. In 1981, I have myself seen a plaque of the sun-god, venerated by the early Arab rulers, kept preserved in the guard room at the old ruines at Hatara in Iraq.

3 "Rubruquais and other travellers."

4 "Colonel Mackenzie's invaluable and gigantic collection."

5 Tod, op.cit., vol. i, pp.481-482. It must however be clarified that no similarity or link with the Indian Aryans has ever been considered admissible by the other Aryans. The former, on their part, till the beginning of this century, did not even shake hands with the latter to

began and later Dravidian monarchs enticed Brahmins through offers of land to settle in their kingdoms to promote culture and religion. Millions of inhabitants of unknown faith were swept off by the new avalanche of Brahmanism and a stage came when the proselytes became more faithful than the pristine propagators and mastered Sanskrit better. Till today the Dravidian Namboodiri priests from down South control the four *dhams* which their pioneer, the Adishankara, founded throughout the length and breadth of India at Badrinath, Puri, Dwarka and Rameshwaram having also established other famous 16 shrines jotted throughout the land apart from Pashupatinath in Nepal.[7] Such has been the greatness displayed by the Aryan Brahmins that they let the freshers run the show. Brahmanism must have had a fall; how else is one to understand that the Brahmins of the South, who had regained hold over the Buddhists, when their counterparts in the North had lost the intellectual battle, were later shunned by their own disciples. Is that not why the DMK which emerged in 1930, asked for sterner measures against the Brahmins even to the extent of demanding a separate *Dravidistan*? Hatred crossed all bounds so much so that E.V.R. Naicker, the movement's prime exponent, commanded his followrs, "If you see a Brahmin and a snake together, kill the Brahmin first". Had the Brahmins not become arrogant and self-seeking, perhaps such animosity would not have emerged. It is unfortunate that the *guru* himself espoused apartheid and that till as late as in 1948, in South India the dividing line

---

keep away from 'defilement'!

6 H.G. Rawlinson, op.cit., pp.12-13.

7 The late Mr. K.P.S. Menon was asked by me after his lecture in 1966 that when the great Adishankara (born in Malabar about A.D. 788) could reunite the whole of India under Hinduism, how it was that Kailash and Mansarovar were left excluded. Mr. Menon, then about 80, smilingly replied that Adishankara's life was cut short when he was but 32. Had he lived longer he might have visited Tibet and the question would have been settled forever. As to how the great first Shankaracharya, a *brahmachari* (celibate) of the highest order, won a battle against a theological arbitratrix at a crucial time is shrouded in mystery. What does come out is that our women had access to all the *Vedas* till at least the eighth century which our intransigents denied them later.

between the master and the pupil was exhibited as a notice outside public restaurants "For Brahmins only" which brought into being a division as deep as the one created by the British of having separate "Hindu *Piao*" and "Muslim *Piao*" (water for public drinking).

As we have seen, in earlier India as well as in Greater India, the Brahmins neither used physical power to convert fresh people nor let prejudice come in the way of their pride and married the local converted women without using any coercion. How these same people forgot their large-heartedness and adopted an insolent attitude towards their own pupil is a sorry chapter. No doubt we have had many invasions. In each war there have to be prisoners and some of them could not resist the pressure demanding relinquishment of one's faith. But when the self-censured man in repentance after release wanted to get rid of the ordeal, he was not forgiven by the Brahmins for having swallowed the bitter beef and was never taken back in the fold. The same egoism percolated down the other classes and worse punishment was reserved for those prisoners who had resisted the pressure and retained their faith in bondage. Upon release, despite grief and regret at having been through captivity, they were never allowed to be their former self and survived only as slaves of their own people, no matter what their earlier status was. Alberuni (died 1039 A.D.) noted, "These Hindus do not desire that a thing once defiled should be readopted after purification ... foolishness is a disease that has no cure. The Hindus believe that there are no people.. no king... no religion... no science that can match theirs... Their predecessors were not so narrow-minded as their present generation". [8] The forced convertee to Islam in his own land was looked down upon by his own people and nobody even cared to have a look even at a *paan* (betal leaf) touched by him. Narcissism became the bane of Hindu society so much so that going abroad and even crossing of the seas was banned forgetting their earlier exploits around the world.

Now we are told that the Brahminical order brought orthodoxy

---

[8] *Kitabul Hind*; E.A. Sachau, *Alberuni's India*, London 1888.

in sex as late as in the middle ages. If that was so it would not have succeeded against Buddhism. The reason for its ascendancy over Buddhist supremacy in the earlier stages is attributed to the revolt it led against the freedom exhibited the *bhikkus* and nuns in the Buddhist *viharas* where gross sensuality and carnal passions of man had found religious sanction resulting in a looseness of sexual morality masquerading in the name of religion. Unbridled licentiousness brought odium upon the whole Buddhist religion and hastened its decline. The ruthless massacre of Buddhists by Sultan Altamash (1211-36) was the finishing blow that led to its exit from India.

The relevant fact is that whereas in the middle ages after Buddhism, orthodoxy was brought in by the Brahmins in many other fields but in matters related to sex some of them became indulgent. The worst havoc was played by some who had the priestly power thrust upon them as a hereditary right without having any intellecutal backing. Greed and lust obscured their view to a greater extent than even at the time of the rise of Buddhist and Jain rebellions earlier, for then at least carnal passions did not play any part as these revolts were basically seeking reforms against excessive ritualism and were designed to eradicate priestcraft and animal sacrifice. Debasement in matters of sex got exposed to view later in some big temples. This vagarity should however not make us forget that in their earlier mission the Brahmins had always maintained a serene and humane approach. Their conduct has been in sharp contrast to the means adopted by victorious people of some other faiths who held no bars in inflicting inhuman punishment on disobedient infidels. Hands have been chopped off, hair lock have been pulled to shear off the scalp, the intransigent have been boiled in a broiler or walled up alive and even crucification has been resorted to. In most cases women have been made the worst scapegoats. The easiest way had been rape and then murder of the helpless unwilling females. Man's bestiality and heartlessness however knew no bounds to find other ignominious methods. We have seen how the charming bosoms are the nursery of human love. We should not fail to see how their fall was brought by man. '"In the fifteenth century, Jewish martyrs were suspended

suspended by their breasts by cords or ropes looped around their breasts".[9] Whether this agony was meant to be final or temporary is not known.

Let us see another havoc that menfolk brought on a brave captive soul. How much agony is caused when one hears of the shameful indignities the great Joan of Arc (1412-31) was subjected to, when she was captured and put on to a trial by the English in collusion with the bought over antagonist French religious order, on being told that Tommies were made to visit her every day and night relentlessly in her captivity. Yet, hardly 18, she kept up her brave spirit of defiance till she was burnt at the stake as a witch. Can we blame some Frenchmen for having a disrespect for religion? Her being canonised in 1919 has hardly made a difference in their outlook.

Be it said to the credit of the Brahmins that when the invaders did come, as much desirous of land, loot and women as of converting the infidel, the former continued to inspire their followers to refuse to accept the shelter offered by the new faith and live defiantly, even woefully, under the sword of Damocles hanging over their head. As for the invaders, they were faced with harsh options. Rawlinson says, "Being far away from home, they knew there was no retreat. They must conquer or die... The early Mohammedan invaders were fierce and bigoted and looked upon it as a right to plunder and enslave the Hindus, and a religious duty to destroy the temples and idols. But as time went on, things began to change. Mohammedans began to intermarry with Hindu woman, and the children of these marriages were more tolerant in their outlook. Hindus of the lower castes were converted to Islam, but retained many Hindu customs, such as not eating beef or allowing widows to remarry. Hindus adopted many Mohammedan social customs, ceremonial and dress and started the practice of keeping women behind the *purdah*." [10] Instinct for survival, which had

---

9 Hebrew manuscripts; Kohut, *Geschichte der deutschen Juden*, Berlin, 1896; Women, op.cit., vol.i, p.453.

10 Rawlinson, op.cit., p.132-134.

forced the poor and the low classes to get absolved from paying the dreaded *jezya* tax, also came into action in other ways. During famines, many a *dhattianis* had to be offered in a *doli* (bride) to the Muslim landlords in Sind, whether new setters or those converted to Islam via Budhism since Mahomed Bin Kasim's days, so that adequate quantity of foodgrains was obtained as a reward for the rest of the family to subsist. The worst pressure was encountered when demand was made on land itself; unless a *doli* was offered, the poor conquered beast had to part with it. When even Manu had advised his followers to guard their land at any cost, could these helpless beings be blamed if they chose the lesser disaster?

Later, due to Brahmins' individualism, the British had to reduce their number from the native regiments because few would eat 'contaminated' food from the common *langar* cooked by another person even if he belonged to their class. Finally a word of warning was given by Col. Tod who was Chanakya (Kautilya) Toynbee and V.P. Menon combined of his age: "*Hindust'han* abounds with Brahmins, who make excellent soldiers, as far as bravery is a virtue; but our officers are cautious, from experience, of admitting too many into a troop or company, for they still retain their intriguing habits. I have seen nearly as many of the Brahmins as of military in some companies; a dangerous error."[11]

How one so outspoken in his appreciation of the Brahmanical order, whose wide vision scanned throughout the universe in search for their hidden greatness, who masterminded most of the treaties which the British ratified with most of the Indian princes, whose erudite research work is a masterpiece which should be the text book of anyone ambitious for any seat of power in India, could revolt against his own inspiration is something that should not be ignored. When lay-brahmins, whom Manu called elephants made of wood, had greatness thrust upon them and began to pilot our destiny, the edifice built on solid foundations laid by their erudite predecessors started crumbling. Now, with passage of time, our seers and sages have again withdrawn into oblivion. If Valmikis

---

[11] Tod, op.cit., vol.i, p.24.

and Vyases have disappeared, as also Annie Besants, Gandhi, Azads and Ambedkars, can we blame the Moghuls or the British for this? Should we then not listen to the enlightened ones, of any caste, creed, colour or nationality, who are the real Brahmins of the day?

Unfortunately the intellectuals in our midst do not care to apply their energies for the general good like the Brahmins of yore. Of the four pillars of Estate, luckily we have got rid of monarchy and its manifestation in minor princelings. As for our clergy, the less said the better. One of the four Shankaracharyas, can still have the gumption to supports *Sati* and favour the ban on entry of *Harijans* in the temples. Silence of the other three *Jagadgurus*, the incarnations of the Adishankara, is more indicative of their acquiescence, if not of mere apathy. The third pillar, Parliament, no doubt still attracts some talented persons, yet its roots have been soiled in corruption.When, to get into this august assembly a person has to spend millions, by begging, borrowing or extortion, in defiance of all laws, then the whole parameter of his activities gets confined to his desire to get back what he has, if at all, himself invested, repay by all foul means imaginable those who betted on the winning horse and build sufficient reserves for the future. To expect that these small time politicians, who have waded through the moat of corruption and bigotry to seats of power, would have any desire to safeguard the interest of those whom they represent is asking for the moon. The first thing they do is to forget the basic difference between being a representative or a delegate and thus murder democracy, and pass only those laws that suit them.

As for the intellectuals, our lawyers always dominated the national struggle for freedom. If they can go on an indefinite strike in Delhi in defence of their rights and continue with it even after the logo gets exposed as a sexual paranoid, what prevents them to take a stand against crimes against women? It is no doubt heartening to note that their counterparts in Bombay can muster immesurable verve to sweep out moral recession reported to have set in our judiciary even up to the High Court level. The resolutions passed by the Lawyers Associations of Bombay in June 90, virtually charging some judges of the High Court with corruption, is a move unprecedented in the history of any modern democracy. The lawyers know more facts of a case than even the judges. They also know that, "Evil is more infectious than AIDS and, if unchecked, progresses with an inevitable momentum of its own". [12] Should not then our lawyers refuse to defend those criminals whose complicity in cases of dowry deaths or rape cannot remaind hidden from them, and also expose these offenders after ascertaining all the details?

Our doctors in hospitals are too preoccupied with their professional or material advancement, if not more busy with the nurses instead of patients. Our highest judiciary does distinguish itself in imparting justice but does it have the authority to ensure that its judgments are carried out? Our students, who were always in the forefront of all struggles, are now nowhere in the combat for betterment of our women. And our teachers, as always, are languishing in their own poverty. In fact there is hardly any movement which can make itself felt against social evils.There is need for a rejuvenated Brahmanism to emerge not only to wipe off present stagnation but to put a halt to the downward march being advocatd in the twin garb of modernism as well as chauvinism.

With the callous attitude being displayed by those who can enforce some order, the Fourth Estate remains the only symbol of hope to salvage our society from the marsh engulfing us. Yet, more often than not, it is just content to play the passive role of only disseminating the alarming events in brief columns. Few articles are written by eminent journalists demanding action against those who condone, overlook or hide such crimes which have reduced our better halves to be mute spectators of their suffering. One has to see to believe how much uproar is created, and space devoted, by the whole American Press today, even in city newspapers, say Chicago Tribune on each case of infringement of social rights of women, howsoever minor. Where is the verve of the cursade launched by the Indian Press during the struggle for

---

[12] Nani A. Palkhiwala, *Times of India*, 9 Jul., 90.

our freedom? Was not freedom also meant for our women ? Why do not these moulders of mass opinion, some of whom are as good as any in the world, agitate and mobilise people to burn the citadels of evil? No state-controlled radio or TV will. Why should this intelligentsia not cut across party lines and religious barriers and create such a furore that those in seats of power are shaken so badly that they pay some attention to heal the wounded womb? We all have come through the same passage and it is our duty to ensure that it is not corroded any further. Let the Press vindicate the promise conveyed in the *Bhagwad-Gita* that the Supreme spirit incarnates itself when the need arises.[13]

---

[13] Bhagwad-Gita IV.7.

24

WHERE DO WE GO

Soon after the Union Jack was brought down from the ramparts of the Red Fort, Toussaint made the observation: "The states that today go to make up India proper continue to show such diversity that it could well endanger the future of Indian unity, which, as we recall, did not come into being until fairly recently and because of a foreign influence, that of the British administrators. Not very long ago, Andre Siegfried noted that the expression 'the Indies' was still valid... Lack of unity has always been an old ailment of the Eastern world... How is it possible to imagine that a state of things that has existed for so long can be radically changed between one day and the next?... Whether they want to or not, the only way the Eastern peoples can recover their strength is not by opposing Europe but, on the contrary, by becoming more and more Europeanised, without, in so doing, giving up their individuality"... [1]

Good and sincere piece of advice. However, the overriding stipulation in the quest for progress is 'without giving up one's individuality'. This advice, to become Europeanised, given in general for the recovery of our strength, is also being advocated by some of our avant-gardes who want us to follow it in the social sphere forgetting whether the Europeans themselves desire a change in their pattern of life or we need to give up our individuality in its entirety.

We are not a new society. There is nothing in the delicate matters of human relations that is not known to us. Our age-old manifold scriptures and texts have covered the subject of life and sex in all totality, clearly delineating duties of man and woman. We have had a look at the life led by women in earlier times in India as well as in some other parts of the world. One can safely say that

---

[1] Toussaint, op.cit., pp.241-243.

life of women in India then was better than anywhere else though of course one cannot claim that our women were enjoying completely equal status with men. In the vast superabundance of Hindu religious texts some inner contradictions are also traced on the subject. When different texts are written over a period of milleniums, with each sage expounding his solution to a situation obtaining at a particular time, there are bound to be differences. The disheartening thing to note, as we have seen, is that when two earlier contemporaries like Manu and Kautilya gave divergent views, those that were more favourable to women were kept clamped down for centuries and when these saw the light of the day hardly any notice was taken of them. Manu did and still reigns supreme. Fair enough. Is it then not a matter of concern that only those edicts of Manu which demand control on women are given publicity, while others which show her the way to live on her feet , like the one exhorting her to live the life of a spinster instead of agreeing to be tied in matrimonial knots to an undesirable person or the one which allows a young girl to find her own mate if her father is unable to get a suitable one, are kept in the dust-bin? The wrost havoc was played by those 'sages' who deprived our women, the right to read even the scriptures. Gradually they, our women, were denied basic education as it was considered an unnecessary luxury that would come in the way of their lives as good house-wives! Various invasions of course forced us to keep our women behind, away from the evil eye, even to the extent of their being withdrwn in the cage of *zenana*. Yet, despite all the vicissitude, the overall picture of woman that emerges is of her being kept under strict male control, required to lead a chaste life. And on her doing so, she was given the best of respects and treated as an adviser on all major issues concerning the family.

People elsewhere who have gone through subjugation have rebelled against it and after overthrowing it have marched forward giving their women the right to assert themselves and find their rightful place in the social structure. Women have also not been found wanting in making their contribution. The Jews, who have gone through the worst of gas chambers, have now entrenched themselves in Israel. Their womenfolk are today fighting shoulder to shoulder with their men and are significantly instrumental in safeguarding their acquisition. And can we, Indian men, who gained our independence more than 40 years ago, who have marched forward in many fields, honestly say that we have given a fair chance to our women to make their contribution? In order to bring our present day deranged life back to order should we not, as a start invigorate our age-old tired-out regulations so that our women at least regain their honour? But then these days, many times in a mistaken view, anything of earlier times is considered as worthless, all old ideas are condemned as retrograde and talk of women's honour viewed as a subterfuge to keep them back.

I am not a bigot. I am not against progress. I am not a traditionalist or a counter-revolutionary who feels that by giving honour alone one can shelve the issue. I look forward to growth and seek its ways whether in the past, present or future. I am fully aware that some people have everywhere been allergic to any progress made by the young.When the Aswan dam was to be built in Egypt , some old scriptures in stone were found which could not be translated. An Egyptologist was called for from England who aftter six months of research deciphered what was just a lecture given by a professor of Alexandria University in the early twelfth century, the opening sentence of which was that, "The younger generation is going to dogs". The younger generation never did so and is today reaching greater heights. As a child I used to call the moon, *Chand Mama* (Uncle Moon!). Now the present generation has landed there unveiling it as a barren land thereby setting aside innumerable myths about its mystical powers; that distance still lends enchantment to the view is a different matter. All athelectic records are getting broken and bettered day by day. This does call for rejoicing. At the same time have we not to be cautious that one does not take the help of drugs unheard of earlier? Should not progress, therefore, aim to achieve betterment without our taking recourse to measures that produce side effects which eclipse the very purpose? Evolution in reality cannot bring about dramatic changes overnight. We have seen how sudden changes brought out in the social sphere in the USA, the USSR and China have brought repugnant repercussions therein without even bringing out economic equality for both the sexes. Should we then not first regain what we lost earlier and then consolidate our gains to embark on a steady path of progress?

We may take pride in the fact that we, the only bipeds, are a better class than any other living being as the other nearest form of existence, chimpanze, a quadruped, has a full form of intelligence equal to that of a human child of only one year's age. We may also take pleasure in knowing that whereas in the case of lower forms of life, the gestation period is limited to an ordained period fixed by nature, written down as dictated by their genes whereby they breed only at a certain period of the year, in human beings, there is hardly any such restriction except for the menstrual cycle unique to a human female. If God has given us greater latitude to have sexual pleasure, does it mean that we get engrossed in this game in time and out of time with anyone available even if the object or the method is not regular and fall a prey to abominations? Are we to reduce ourselves to a level that is lower than even that of the animals and let sex dominate all our activities? Let us not forget what the *Vishnu Purana* says, "The society decays when property confers rank; wealth becomes the only basis of virtue, passion the sole bond of union between man and woman, falsehood the source of success in life, sex the sole means of enjoyment, when the outer trappings are mistaken for the inner spirit". [2]

The interplay of cultures is no doubt of significance to the whole world. Integration of culture, however, does not imply the surrender and merging of one culture into another. Kipling may have expressed the innermost feelings in many a colonialist when he said, "Oh, East is East and West is West, and never the twain shall meet", partly to remind his fellowmen of the superiority of pre-mutiny their race, partly to show his disapproval of the easy way of life adopted by his countrymen, each keeping their share of *bibis* as well as patronising the native *nautch* girls, *hookah* and *kurta* particularly in the pre-mutiny period, as also to tell them that in

---

[2] IV. 24.21-22. *Radhakrishnan's E.T. in Indian Philosophy II*, p.665; *Gandhi and Social Sciences*, op.cit., p.46.

in dealing with the natives, unless the stiff upper lip was kept, the Empire would be lost. However, he himself mixed with courtesans like Lalun, with Jewish freemasons, with *fakirs*, with bazaar loafer, with private soldiers and with any native that would talk to him. His contempt for Indian culture is scarcely a reflection of any indepth study.[3] Instead we may quote one speaking with conviction and known to have profound knowledge. Says Max Müller, "If one would ask me under what sky the human mind has most fully developed its precious gifts, has scrutinised most profoundly the greatest problems of life, and has at least for some, provided solutions which deserve to be admired even by those who have studied Plato and Kant, I would indicate India. And if one would ask me which literature would give us back (us Europeans who have been exclusively fed on Greek and Roman thought and on that of a Semitic race) the necessary equilibrium in order to make our inner life more perfect, more comprehensive, more universal, in short, more human, a life not only for this life, but for a transformed and eternal life, once again I would indicate India."[4]

Let us, however, not get unnecessarily elated. Let us ask ourselves honestly, whether our actions today make us deserve these compliments paid to our ancients. Our society, like any other, has it good points as well as its defects. Let us then give heed to the advice of Mr. H.C. Chakladar, formerly Head of the Department of

---

[3] A stage came when his countrymen did not care to remember the last two lines of the same stanza, given below, as perhaps no strong man was left to stand face to face:

THE BALLAD OF EAST AND WEST

Oh, East is East, and West is West,
    and never the two shall meet,
Till Earth and Sky stand presently at
    God's great Judgment Seat;
But there is neither East nor West,
    Border, nor Breed, nor Birth,
When two strong men stand face to
    face, tho' they come from the ends
    of the earth.

[4] *The Cultural Heritage of India*, op. cit., vol.iv, p.28; *India — What*

Anthropology, Calcutta University:

"There is need, however, to guard against false spirituality—against inactivity and sloth, passivity and feebleness, which not infrequently masquerade as spirituality... Added to this internal decay, there is an inrush of external forces that has thrown us off our feet. The aggressive civilisation of the West... has caught us in its iron grip. Many of us... would even unthinkingly introduce in our midst institutions that the best thought in the West has found defective and even harmful... Contact with Western life for over a century has now made it amply clear that the modern European or American life has its bright and dark aspects, equally with the present-day Hindu life. At this juncture we require a searching analysis of both the civilisations... A comparative study of the two cultures by and for the Indians has become a vital necessity. Let us hope that this very struggle with an alien civilisation will impart new life and vigour to us. Let this stimulus from without advance our growth, not retard it."[5]

In all fairness we must accept that the greatest service that the Western society has done to humanity is to let their woman grow up as an independent individual who has all the opportunities available to her, who can plan her mode of life and can look after herself on her own. This of course has not been a smooth passage. It is the result of a long-drawn out struggle which is still continuing to remove the existing shortcomings. Must we force our women to take up the same struggle from scratch and go through all the ordeals just to be treated as human beings ?

We have at the very beginning of this work seen how Dr. Annie Besant described Indian womanhood in its pristine form. Noble sentiments these, but our social set-up has to some extent moved forward since the time these were expressed. Today, our educated womanhood, particularly in the major cities, is not inclined to let itself be divided as earlier in the concept of being

---

can it teach us ? Lectures at Cambridge University, 1882, Longmans, Green and Co., London, 1905; Munshi Ram Manohar Lal, Delhi.

[5] H.C. Chakladar, *The Cultural Heritage of India*, op. cit., vol.ii, p.580.

either a Savitri [6] sitting at home, or classified as accessible when working outside. Some women are marching forward proving that they can rise to any heights in any field. In my morning walks, I see a thousand young girls going to their different schools, their school dresses unwittingly showing their standard of living. But on each face there is a hope of a better tomorrow. Instead of their future being confined to be a nurse, a typist or steno, a receptionist or a hotel house-keeper, they would prefer that they are not denied the opportunity available to their brothers of being a doctor, an executive, a manager, a director or an administrator. Even if they have to live as housewives they would like to have full benefits of education so that they bring up their children better. One does not know which one of them may get the inspiration to be an Annie Besant or a Sarojini Naidu. Has not, despite a woman not being allowed to be a priest, Mother Teresa shown us her most brilliant luminescence? How long we propose to, or think we can, curtail our women's aspirations?

As regards relationship with the other sex, almost none of the Indian girls wants to live the life of a spinster. Those who are divorcees or become widows also wish to re-enter conjugal harmony. There is no desire for lesbianism and hardly any for free sex. One cannot of course rule out that as time passes and more Indian women get educated they would react more strongly on seeing their rivals in polygamy, adultery or homosexuality. Ergo, one wonders whether today those who are calling for removal of all sexual inhibitions are really representing the interests of India's women or expressing women's innermost desire or as a cover plan are advocating the cause of the frustrated Indian male. Let us hope the Indian women will themselves speak out on the subject.

Arnold Toynbee, the celebrated author of twelve fat volumes under the title; *A Study of History* thundered some years ago in one

---

[6] In the story of Savitri of the *Mahabharat* era we have the ideal wife. In her youth she was so exquisitively beautiful and had such an aureole of dignity about her that no young man would venture to seek her hand in marriage. Her name is remembered because she wrenched her husband from *Yama*, the son of the Sun, the god of death.

of his addresses in the University of Edinburgh: "In fifty years the world would be under the hegemony of the United States but in the twenty first century, as religion captures the place of technology, it is possible that India, the conquered, will conquer its conquerors".[7]

What religion is Toynbee referring to? Religion that gives our woman a right to live as equals or a religion that ties them down in shackles? We have seen that more atrocities have been committed on woman throughout the world in the name of religion than on any other account. We also cannot hide the fact that in their struggle for survival some religious bigots are insistent in retaining not only the initial known shortcomings but also the ugly distortions brought in later by unscrupulous priesthood. What prevents us today to modify or remove those facets which are coming in the way of progress of half of humanity?

Reforms have always added laurels to the glory of religion and never curtailed it. Can anyone say that by our bringing out some changes like giving a share to our daughters in the property of their father, by making an effort to prevent child marriages and *sati* by law, by granting our women equal right to divorce, by allowing our widows to remarry, there has been any diminution in the radiance of Hindu religion? On the other hand our refusal to take timely corrective measures would have only brought ridicule and revulsion for it. At the same time let us be honest to ourselves. How many of these reforms are being truthfully observed by the people at large and how many try to get around considering these as unnecessary?

We have not yet made a determined effort to find out and enforce what initially had been acknowledged to be right. As Mr. Justice Gajendragadkar highlighted, "Perhaps, in course of time other works on *Artha-Sastra* may be discovered... Unfortunately, during the British rule, Hindu law has not been studied 'from

---

[7] Huston Smith, The Religion of Man, p.25; Gandhi and Social Sciences, op.cit., p.46.

within', with the help of Sanskrit Texts. As the Privy Council observed in the case of Collector of Madura v. Mooto Ramalinga, the duty of a judge administering Hindu law was not 'so much to enquire whether a disputed doctrine is fairly deducible from the earliest authority, as to ascertain whether it has been received by the particular school which governs the District with which he has to deal.'[8] This apporach imposed limitation on judges, and in the administration of Hindu law... for a proper study of Hindu law, its origin, growth, and development, it would be necessary to undertake a study of all the Sanskrit texts available on the subject. The relevant literature offers, as Dr. Rash Behari Ghosh observed long ago, a rich and varied field for enquiry. The harvest has been ripening for the sickle, but as yet to our reproach, the reapers are few in number, and the wealth of materials which should be our pride is now our disgrace'.[9]

Two basic questions arise for our men to ponder. Are we to wait for a discovery to be made as to what our ancients said thousands of years ago and accept the rightful approach only if they had so advised? Suppose we do not succeed in the effort, what prevents us from earnestly adopting these measures which we would have called for had we been women ? Secondly, how long are we to remain slaves of our " customs" which continue to form the most important element which governs Hindu law ? Who formed these customs? Was it Vishnu, Brahma, Manu? Weren't it our own people some of whom for diverse reasons lived a deranged life for quite sometime in different regions and who adopted divergent customs to suit their needs at a particular time? Were they any better than us who have a global view and can work out what is best for us? The need of the hour, therefore, is to give our society a shake up so that it purges itself of its errors and regains its social tranquility. Steps should be taken up by us urgently which should allow our social mainstream to wash off the

---

[8] 12 Moore's Ind. App. 397, 436 *The Cultural Heritage of India*, vol. ii, p.432.

[9] Dr. Rash Behari Ghosh, *Law of Mortgages*, IVth Edn., p. 35; P.B. Gajendragadkar, op.cit., p.432.

polluting elements rather than let itself be submerged by them.

In the end, we may remember what Dr. Sir S. Radhakrishnan, for years professor at Oxford and later our President, said of our civilization. "The civilisation which is inspired by the spiritual insight of our sages is marked by a certain moral integrity, a fundamental loyalty, a fine balance of individual desires and social demands, and it is these that are responsible for its vitality and continuity. To a departure from the ideals can be traced the present weakness and disorder of the Hindu civilization."[10] Taking this as a guideline we should chalk out a path that would enable our women to live like human beings. The choice before us is whether we ramain inebriated with inertia or we march forward on a stable path of lasting happiness! We ourselves have to find the answer.

"Know then thyself, presume not God to scan,
The proper study of mankind is man"

Alexander Pope.

---

10 Dr. S. Radhakrishnan, *The Cultural Heritage of India*, op.cit., vol.i, p.xxiii.

BIBLIOGRAPHY

Ainsworth, W.F., *Narative of the Euphrates Expedition*, II.

Alberuni, *Kitabul Hind.*

Besant, Annie, *The Birth of New India; The Commonwealth.*

Brown, Hilton, *The Sahibs*, William Hodge and Co.Ltd., London, 1948.

Bruce, *Travel to discover the source of the Nile*, Edinburgh, 1790.

Burton, Sir Richard F., and Arbuthnot, F.F., *The Kama Sutra of Vatsyayana.*

Childe, V. Gordon, *New light on the Most Advanced East*, Routlege and Kegan Paul, 2nd Edn., London, 1952.

Claret, Archbishop, *Llave de Oro*, Pablo Ricra, 1860.

Coedés, G., *Les Etas hindouisés d'Indochine et d'Indonesie*, Paris, 1948. Collins, Larry; Lapierre Dominique, *Freedom at Midnight*, Vikas, New Delhi, 1976.

Collis, Maurice, *Foreign Mud*, Faber and Faber Ltd., London.

Darwin, Charles, *Essaie sur L' inégalité des races humaines*, Paris, 1853.

Dellon, *Voyages de M. Dellon avec sa relation de l'Inquistition de Goa*, 3 Vols, Cologne, 1711.

Devic, M., *Les Merveilles de l'Inde*, Paris.

Durant, Will, *Our Oriental Heritage*, Simon and Schuster, New York, 1942.

Eldridge, F.B., *The Background of Eastern Sea Power*, London, 1948.

Furber, Holden, *John Company at Work*, Cambridge, Mass, 1952.

Furnivall, *Child Marriages in The Diocese of Charter*, London, 1897.

Galbraith, John Kenneth, *Ambassador's Journal*, Hamish Hamilton, London, 1969.

Gallico, De Bello, *Caesar.*

Gandhi, M.K., *Economics of Khadi*, Navajivan Press, Ahmedabad, 1941.

Greenberg, M., *British Trade and the Opening of China*, 1800-1842, Cambridge, 1951.

Hardy, Thomas, *Tess of the D'Urbervilles*, 1891.

Hirschfeld, M., *Die Homosexualitat des Mannes u.d. Weibes*, Berlin, 1914.

Hite, Shere, *Women and Love*, 1987.

Hoskins, H.L., *British Routes to India*, Frank Cass and Co. Ltd., 1966.

Ibn Shahriyar, *Ajaib al Hind* or *The Wonders of India.*

Iqbal, Dr Sir Muhammed, *The Reconstruction of Religious Thought in Islam*, Lahore, 1960.

Iyer, Sri P.S. Sivaswami, *Evolution of Hindu Moral Ideals*, Kamla Lectures, 1935.

Joint Women's Programme, New Delhi, *The Women's Decade*, 1975-85.
Kebbel, T.E., *Selected Speeches of the Rt. Hon. the Earl of Beaconsfield*, 2 vols., London, 1882.
Kincaid, *Dennis, British Social Life in India.*
Kipling, Rudyard, *The Works of Kipling*, Black's Readers Service Co., New York.
Kohut, *Geschichte der deutschen Juden*, Berlin, 1896.
Lawrence, T.E., *Seven Pillars of Wisdom*, 1926, Jonathan Cape Ltd., London, Jan 46.
Lea, Henry C., *History of Sacerdotal Celibacy in the Christian Church*, London, 1907.
Lerchenfeld, *Das Frauenleiber der Erde*, Wien, Pest, Leipzig 1881.
Maine, *Early Law and Custom*; *Ancient Law.*
Majumdar, R.C., *An Advanced History of India*, London, 1956.
Manucci, Niccolao Venetian, *Storia do Mogor*, Eng. Trans by William Irvine, 1907-08.
Marshall, Sir John, *Mohenjo-daro and the Indian Civilisation.*
Masters, John, *Bugles and a Tiger.*
Mayo, Kathcrine, *Mother India.*
Milton, John, *Paradise Lost.*
Mukherjee, R.K., *Indian Shipping*, Bombay, 1957.
Müller, Max *India — What can it teach us* ? Longman, Green and Co., London, 1905; Munshi Ram Manohar Lal, Delhi, 1961.
Munster, Sabastian, *Cosmographie Oder Beschrubungaller Länder*, Basel, 1548.
Narada, *Stripumsa.*
Natarajan, S., *A Century of Social Reform in India*, Asia Publishing House, Bombay, 1959.
Nehru, Jawaharlal, Collection of important speeches, *Independence and After*, Aug. 1949.
Niem, Theodoricus de, *Hist. Sui, Temporis Libri*, IIII Argentorat, 1609.
Pearsall, Dr Paul, *Super marital sex: Loving for life*, Edbury Press, London, 1987.
Plato, *The Symposium.*
Ploss, Heinrich; Bartels, Max and Paul, *Woman*, William Heinemann (Medical Books) Ltd. 1935; Whitefriars Press Ltd., London, 1935.
Plutarch, *Opera Parisiis*, 1841-1855.
Pope, Alexander, *Rape of the Lock.*
Pradt, Abbé de, *Les Trois Ages des colonies*, Paris, 1902.
Radhakrishnan, Dr. S., *Mahatma Gandhi.*
Ramakrishna Mission Institute of Culture, *The Cultural Heritage of India* , 5 vols; Calcutta, 1975.
Rawlinson, H.G., *A Concise History of the Indian People*, (first

published 1938), Oxford University Press, Madras, seventh impression, 1968.

Ryder, Brainerd, *The Little Wives of India*, Melbourne, 1892.

Sachau, E.A., *Alberuni's India.*

Sadat Jehan, *A Woman of Egypt*, Simon and Schuster, New York, 1987.

Scherr, J., *Duestche Kultre Und Sitterges Chichte*, Leipzing, 1858.

Ségur, Comte, *Les femmes, Leur conditions at leur influence dans l'ordre sociale.*

Shaw, George Bernard, *Getting Married*, Constable and Co. Ltd., London, 1927.

Smith, Huston, *The Religion of Man.*

Stanford, J.K., *Ladies in the Sun*, The Galley Press, London, 1962.

Stead, W.T., The *Maiden Tribute of Modern Babylon*, London, 1885.

Tavernier, J.B., *Travels in India*, London, 1925.

Tod, Colonel James, *Annals and Antiquities of Rajasthan*, 1820.

Tolstoy, Leo, *War and Peace.*

Toussaint, Auguste, *Historire de L'océan Indien*, Presses Universitaires de France, 1961; *History of Indian Ocean*, London 1966.

Toynbee, Arnold, *A Study of History.*

Tuzuk-i-Jahangiri, tran. by Rogers and edited by H. Beveridge, Royal Asiatic Society, London.

Vidyarthi, L.P.; Sahey, B.N.; Srivastava B.K., *Gandhi and Social Sciences*, Council of Social and Cultural Research, Bihar, Bookhive, New Delhi, 1970.

Virey, *Journal Universel des Sciences*, 1816.

Wales, Quaritch, *Pre-history and Religion in South-East Asia*, London, 1957.

Ward, Vide, *On the History, Literature, and Mythology of the Hindus.*

Weinhold, K., *Die Deutchen Frauen in Mettelalater*, Wien, 1882.

Wilkan, G.A., *Das matriarchat bei den alten arabern*, Leipzig, 1884.

Yaksa, *Nirukta* (c.700 B.C.)

Index